☐

GUILT
AND
HEALING

☐

GUILT
and
HEALING

Wilfrid McGreal O Carm

GEOFFREY
CHAPMAN

Geoffrey Chapman
A Cassell imprint
Villiers House, 41/47 Strand, London WC2N 5JE

First published 1994

British Library Cataloguing-in-Publication Data
A catalogue record for this book is available from the British
Library

ISBN 0-225-66686-3

Cover illustration: John Piper, 'The Prodigal Son', from the
Benjamin Britten memorial window in Aldeburgh Church.
Reproduced by courtesy of Mrs John Piper and the Aldeburgh
Bookshop

Author photo by Chris Kelly

Extracts form Mary Gordon, *The Company of Women*
(Jonathan Cape) reproduced by permission of Random House

Typeset by Action Typesetting Ltd, Northgate Street,
Gloucester
Printed and bound in Great Britain by
Biddles Ltd, Guildford and King's Lynn

Contents

Foreword

Guilt, as Wilfrid McGreal makes plain at the outset of this book, is not in itself a negative experience. Indeed, the person who feels no guilt no matter what he or she has done or has failed to do is, psychologically speaking, psychopathic. Such individuals readily yield to impulses, the suppression of which is customary for normal people. The guiltless lack empathy, the ability to enter into the experiences, the feelings of another person. The development of a balanced, healthy, responsible individual, as of society, demands a concept of human guilt. The problem, however, is that for many of us our experience of guilt is not creative and positive, does not serve to turn us from the destructive and enhance our sense of our own potential for goodness but is itself crippling. Much guilt is not an inducement to behave better but a prison which constricts our character and deforms our confidence.

Such has been the power of the Genesis myth, of that dramatic account of man's failure, that in Wilfrid McGreal's view it has actually overshadowed the New Testament message of man's salvation – Adam's sin towers over Jesus' salvation. There is a psychological correlate. Time and time again, psychologists and psychiatrists encounter people who are ground down by a grim, negative, nihilistic self-image. They see themselves as worthless, full of sin and contamination, unable to meet not merely the expectations of others but the insistent, perfectionist demands of their own super-ego. Many people experience life as a constant reminder of what they have been unable to do, of the enormity of the gap between what they hoped they might become and what they perceive themselves to be. They ascribe the responsibility for this failure to their own inadequacies. And they experience a guilt which offers no possibility of redemption, a self-denigration which posits no possibility of recovery.

One of the more regrettable consequences of the particularly Jansenistic form of Christianity in which some of us were educated was the inducement of guilt in relation to normal sexual development – guilt about masturbatory fantasies, guilt about sexual desire, guilt about sexual feelings, guilt about sexual exploration. At the heart of such a view of sexuality is a negative, degrading, fearful view of women. Fr McGreal's analysis does not shirk from exposing this deformity of Christ's message of redemption to critical scrutiny. Unease, anxiety and guilt are, as he powerfully argues, forces for unhappiness and disintegration for many Christians. However, his book insists that this need not be so, that the central message of Christ's teaching is of healing not guilt, of growth not devastation. Healthy people can forgive not only others but themselves too for the basic reality of their humanity, their imperfections. This book goes a long way towards showing us how.

Dr Anthony Clare

□

Introduction

□

This book is the result of a casual conversation that I took seriously. I was on attachment in the summer of 1990 to the Religious Department of the BBC. A colleague, Alistair Simmonds, stopped me in the corridor to discuss ideas for a documentary that could be broadcast on Radio 4. We agreed to mull over ideas about the impact of the thought of the early Fathers on current Christianity. That all seemed quite academic and remote. However, I then chanced upon the recently released paperback of Peter Brown's *The Body and Society*, a powerful study of sexuality and renunciation in the early Church. Brown's book was one that wore its scholarship lightly and reading it helped me make connections. As a priest in pastoral work that has included university chaplaincy, teaching and school chaplaincy, and many years of retreat work, I have come to recognize unease, anxiety and guilt as forces for unhappiness and disintegration among so many Christians and above all Catholics. I went back to Alistair Simmonds and the result of our conversation was the BBC Radio 4 documentary, *The Guilty Party*. The programme was an attempt to look at the sources of guilt, especially among Catholics. We collected an immense amount of information and Alistair's skills as a producer enabled the mass of material to be made manageable. The programme went out co-presented by myself and Dr Anthony Clare in April 1991.

The experience of making the programme and especially Alistair's probing questions led me to think more deeply about guilt and the need for healing. I began to reflect on my own experience as a Carmelite friar and tried to listen more carefully to the people I was working with. Personal circumstances over this period made me evaluate my life more carefully and helped me to see where so many people in the Church were hurting and being hurt. I realized that I was part of that process both as victim and as perpetrator.

Reflecting on my own life I saw so many significant moments that had shaped me and marked me. I can remember a school retreat when I was fourteen. The preacher built up a devastating picture of what would happen to those who broke the sixth and ninth commandments. He pictured our sin, using the image of a body putrefying while the person was alive. During my novitiate we were subject to a handbook on spirituality that was shot through with pessimism. Written by a spartan Bavarian Carmelite, it drew on a rich vein of seventeenth-century pessimism and ignored all that was good in the Carmelite tradition. Student days in pre-Council Rome were also full of inhibiting constraints. Fortunately, over this period of my teens and early religious life, I encountered rich and human characters who lived an alternative vision to all this, and they gave me hope.

The documentary, the questions I was asking and the re-evaluating I was experiencing, have led to a book that wants to do more than rake over old ashes. So many people experience guilt and anxiety, and healing and a road to wholeness has to be found. I would like to help them find a way out of the negative guilt into a healing process.

First of all I would like to stress that guilt or feelings of guilt are not in themselves negative. An absence of guilt in a person's life would be a pathological condition. If I have agreed to give time to a sick person and then cannot be bothered because of laziness, I have clearly behaved in a selfish way. If I begin to feel bad about the situation, I am challenged to do something positive and if I do apologize and make up, then my guilt has brought help and healed the situation. Healthy guilt, as in this case, is a call to responsibility and enables us to grow. However, many people experience guilt linked to anxiety which can be harmful and inhibiting. I would like to look at some of the issues in people's lives that lead to such feelings of

2

guilt and that cannot find an easy resolution. When guilt is unresolved it can too often be crippling and this I find is an all too common experience.

In the first chapter I look at the paradox of Christianity, a religion of truth and freedom and yet a burden for so many people in the Church. Christ in the Gospels is always presented as someone who is accessible, but for people today he can be a distant figure, hidden behind rules and laws.

Recently, when I made a plea for greater pastoral understanding for so many who hurt in the Church, someone reminded me of the danger of shifting ideals so that they were closer to the people – instead, people should do the travelling in order to come closer to the ideals, I was told. I believe that there are moral principles and that most Christians are doing their very best in difficult circumstances to live up to moral principles. They are not asking the Church to change its teaching, but to understand where they are at. Their pleas to those in authority is to be alongside them and help them make sense of the mess, help them feel they belong and above all minister the compassion of Christ to them.

Given the way people feel about their relationships to the Church, the tone and style of the Church's moral teaching becomes extremely important. Church documents come couched in language that needs a great deal of unpacking. The philosophical presuppositions behind so many official pronouncements are often culturally alien to the mind-set of the English-speaking world. This sets up whole areas of possible misunderstanding both by the average member of the Church and even more by the media. In Chapter 2 I have tried to show that the tone and style of Catholic teaching has done little to help people achieve personal growth. The way original sin is presented can lead us to believe that the human race is a disaster and we are all potential failures. I believe that we become fully human when we allow God freedom in our lives and allow grace to fulfil our nature. I also believe that a key way to come to healing is to move from being dominated by the super-ego, which is so often directed towards correctness and approval-seeking behaviour, to a life directed by conscience. The super-ego keeps us introverted and isolated, whereas conscience is dynamic and extrovert. It is directed to discovering values

3

and responds to the invitation to love. Above all it has a community-directed dimension. Being guided by conscience is not being dominated by how we feel about situations; it is a process of deciding what we should do, and also it enables us to review our actions and pronounce on their moral goodness. Conscience presupposes reflection and a desire to be informed. A good way of reflecting is the 'see, judge, act' approach. This entails taking the Scriptures and looking at Christ's response to situations and then applying the analysis to our own lives. If we have sincerely worked at informing our conscience, listening to the Scripture in our hearts and letting Gospel values be our ideal, then we should not be anxious about the decisions we make as a result.

Morality, what is right and wrong, is usually thought about in the area of personal behaviour, and much attention is paid to sexual activity. But issues of morality in the fast-moving world of business are not so easy to identify. The expression 'structural sin' is used more and more to indicate ways in which society in general, and many organizations in particular, act contrary to principles of morality. If some commercial activity is against human dignity then it is wrong, it is sinful. How can men and women in the business world be helped to take responsibility for what happens? Is there such a thing as corporate guilt and how do we bring healing to the world of commerce? Business activities are vital for society; but how they operate matters. Business ethics is a crucial discipline and has done much to check the misuse of power in commerce. However, clever and cynical practices can exist and these cause immense damage to all those who are caught up in them. What does the medical adviser to a manufacturing company do when he finds workers' health is being sacrificed for profit in the company's Third World operations? He is guilty of something he is not entirely responsible for. So what should he do? Again, in the new world order, new responsibilities arise. Have we the imagination to react in a creative manner so that we move away from national or regional self-interest to a sense of caring for our planet? In Chapter 3 I am not in the business of blaming any group or individual but rather I am asking questions to stimulate debate, so that individuals can flourish in all their dignity.

Introduction

Guilt is not always something we rightly feel: often it is imposed on us. Sadly, those who want to preserve the *status quo*, who want to stay in power, do so by making people who are working for change feel that what they are doing is wrong and in this way they impose guilt on the less fortunate. Women are one such group that have guilt imposed on them and so I have called Chapter 4 'Guilty of being a woman' because I believe Church and society consciously or unconsciously impose guilt on women. Women seem to have higher expectations put on them than men, and the pressure of trying to realize them can be death-dealing. I have used passages from contemporary literature to illustrate this. Wherever a woman turns, it would seem she can be criticized. If she works she is neglecting her children. Single parents are targets for right-wing politicians' indignation, and are regarded as a drain on society. They may be made to feel guilty if they look after their children and do not work. A woman is even blamed for the Fall. In Scripture, maleness seems to be the norm for priesthood and as a result a woman's physical nature shuts her off from responsibility for the sacred. I believe that for the good of society and the Church this imposed guilt has to be healed. Why should people's destiny be defined by their anatomy?

In the Carmelite tradition we have learnt that, to be alive and able to speak to our contemporaries, we have had to make our original vision find new life and new ways of expression down the centuries. An inspiration can too quickly become a routine, and therefore I believe every generation has to use its imagination and creativity to bring life to traditions. With this in mind, how can we imagine the Gospel so that what is handed on incarnates Christ's vision for now? I believe that the contemplative tradition of respectful listening is what we need to bring healing into relations between women and men. We need to listen to each other in Church and society so that we can seek forgiveness for past hurts and learn alternatives. The Church is meant to be a counter-culture, not in the sense of saying no to everything in society, but by discerning what is good and what must be opposed. I believe the Christian community can make suggestions as to how we could live together and learn from each other without being threatened.

5

Protest does not mean taking up a superior moral line as if the Church knows better. It may be the fruit of suffering and loss. A community of wounded healers is more likely to speak to a needy world and would be a faithful imaging of its founder. Jesus saved us when broken, and it is in our brokenness that we speak to and heal each other.

People who feel fragile and are buffeted by life can readily reach out for something solid to hold on to. When we are under pressure, threatened and exhausted, we can yearn for some place where we are secure, where decisions are made for us and we can sink into a blissful sleep. There are times when the whole project of life can seem too much and we would like to abdicate and let someone else take charge. Fundamentalism can sometimes present itself as the cure for everything we find difficult in life. I have entitled Chapter 5 'The quick fix' because fundamentalism can seem to answer all our worries. I believe, however, that fundamentalism is an insidious form of control and does little to encourage growth in wholeness. Certainly it is too often concerned with endorsing a political *status quo* and can be a force to buttress unjust structures. The cure can be, in the end, worse than the original problem.

The chapter entitled 'A vision of wholeness' could seem ambitious. Here, I am looking at two ways of guilt and healing: psychological insights and counselling on the one hand and the Church's celebration of reconciliation on the other. What I envision is a way of relating therapy and the Christian life. Both entail commitment and each in its own way can help personal growth. Forgiveness is at the heart of Christianity, and it is this message of the creative change that can happen to us as persons that I want to explore. I believe that Confession as a sacrament has been experienced too often as a narrowly judgemental event rather than the healing force it is meant to be. Confession, or the sacrament of reconciliation, is part of the process of Christian conversion. It is not just a time when we go before a priest to ask for absolution but, more importantly, it enables us to deepen our basic turning to Christ and to recognize when in our lives we need the gift of grace to gain strength and to journey in faith. But conversion, change, all need time, patience and the fullest possible harnessing of all our personal resources. Grace builds on nature; hence my wish to see a fuller interfacing of sacramental and psychological insights.

As I have written this book I have been influenced by others who have trodden different sections of the path. Gabriel Daly's *Creation and Redemption* has helped me make greater sense of a contemporary expression of the doctrine of original sin. Kevin Kelly, both in his writings and in conversation, has shown the importance of an approach to morality that values the basic worth of the individual. I felt less hesitant about writing the chapter 'Guilty of being a woman' after listening to Mary Grey and also reading her book *The Wisdom of Fools?* I read *The Wisdom of Fools?* deep in the bush in Tanzania while I was giving a retreat to the clergy of the Mahenge diocese. As with any book, friends and colleagues influence the writing: Jo McGuigan, with whom I have collaborated for many years in university chaplaincy and retreat work; Loretta Brennan, who enabled me to make sea changes in my thinking, and my Carmelite confrères who listen. Finally, thanks to Clare Abbotson, who translated my script into clarity.

1

□

The paradox of freedom and the driven

□

'The truth will set you free' is a Gospel value that we all readily accept. But does the Christian message bring people to a state of freedom and a sense of integrity? Jesus was hailed as one who spoke with authority. Jesus' authority was his clarity of teaching, cutting through the legalism of his day and thus making the law accessible to everyone who heard him. He insisted that he came not to abolish the law but to fulfil it. The law for Jesus was summed up in the greatest of the commandments: 'You must love the Lord your God with all your heart, with all your soul, with all your strength, and with all your mind, and your neighbour as yourself' (Luke 10:27); but it was also set against the radical manifesto that he proclaimed in the synagogue at Nazareth (Luke 4:16 – 19):

> He came to Nazara, where he had been brought up, and went into the synagogue on the sabbath day as he usually did. He stood up to read, and they handed him the scroll of the prophet Isaiah. Unrolling the scroll he found the place where it is written:
>
>> The spirit of the Lord has been given to me, for he has anointed me.
>> He has sent me to bring the good news to the poor, to proclaim liberty to captives and to the blind new sight, to set the downtrodden free, to proclaim the Lord's year of favour.

Jesus upheld the law, but in the context of proclaiming the Kingdom of his Father reigning in our midst. The truth, mercy, justice and peace of God were the values that would shape human lives, and the structures so long sanctioned by tradition were seen to be at variance with the values of the Kingdom. Power, control and the rule of fear, so long the apparatus of society and empire, were no longer to be important. When Jesus finished his mission he left a community of disciples whose task was to proclaim and establish his Kingdom in the lives of men and women. The early Christian community was a radical group with a radical message. In fact, the first Christians were a serious threat to society because they saw freedom as the primary message of the Gospel. Jesus' death on the cross was a triumph of loving obedience. The victory of the cross rejected all the values that make other systems fearsome, exploitative and power-centred. Jesus was establishing an order of freedom based on an obedience flowing from love.

To live the values that emerge from the Gospel needs radical change in the lifestyle of disciples. This is indeed the call that Jesus makes through the Gospel down the ages: 'Repent, live the Gospel and set your heart on the treasure that is beyond all price.' The disciple is invited to find freedom in trusting in the Father's providence and he or she is promised a hundredfold reward in this life. The context of life is resurrection: there is the realism that suffering will be part of life but so will happiness, fulfilment and pleasure. Christ invites disciples to a way of life that is guided by teaching such as that of the Beatitudes. What is absent from the Gospel is moralizing and rules. The relationship with God that Jesus sets up is one of trust in the Abba, Father. Wonder, simplicity and spontaneity are the reactions of the disciples to God's mercy and power in their lives.

The vision that the Gospel gives of the Christian way of life is demanding, challenging, but life-enhancing. There is no hint of a narrow, legal approach to behaviour. The Father is shown as exercising his power in loving mercy and the great sign of the Kingdom breaking out among men and women is healing. Healing of broken bodies and the forgiveness of sins go hand in hand. Rejoicing over a sinner converted is the sound that rings out. Anxiety is not high on the agenda and if Levi or Zacchaeus admit they are sinners, exploiting the poor, they do something about it. Levi leaves his office, Zacchaeus makes restitution. The women that men regard as bad find acceptance and forgiveness from Christ. His anger is directed towards narrow judgemental minds. What really corrupts is not external behaviour and failures but pride, like an acid that is eating away in the hearts of those who are scarcely living. The Gospel, in saying these things, paints powerful pictures, which bring back the memory of the ministry of Jesus. There is another vital element in its story-telling. The Gospel writers selected many episodes and incidents to reflect the early Church's concerns and the issues that were *live* in the communities for whom the Gospels were written. Many early Christians had been Pharisees, so the tendency to put orthodoxy and correctness at the top of the agenda had to be challenged.

The Gospels and the New Testament as a whole give us a positive message about human behaviour. Christ's saving work has made us a new creation and we are to become God's work of art. Belief expresses itself in a way of relating to people with integrity, and this points to the loving relationship God wants with us. We can redeem the now, and yet our ultimate hope lies in the resurrection. It's true we do not conform to the norms of society, but the life of Christians is one of good open relationships with a deep respect for each other's dignity. Our dignity in turn is rooted in the intimacy that God wants to achieve in us. This vision expresses itself in positive choices: there is no going back to living by a catalogue of prohibitions.

How far does the message of freedom and positive change envisaged by the Gospel express itself in the lives of Christians today? Here a paradox emerges: the people who should have a sense of freedom and responsibility so often seem driven, anxious and burdened with a type of guilt that can only be described as neurotic. The hallmark of many Christians, and especially Catholics, is a sense of guilt which seems to enslave them and has the effect of stunting their development as persons. Guilt in this context has been described as 'a hundred-headed monster'. Why is there such a split between the Gospel and how people feel about themselves and life? Where did the rot set in?

In pastoral work, I find people anxious, driven and guilty in a whole host of situations. However, underlying these attitudes there is the problem of how they envisage their relationship to God. It seems, too often, that God is an angry parent, someone who has to be pleased, and pleasing God is well-nigh impossible, as parents could never be placated. God as a lover, as the one who rejoices at the salvation of the sinner, does not figure.

For some people, pleasing God is achieved by performing rituals, saying certain prayers, attending devotions or going frequently to confession to rid themselves of sin. The problem with this way of expressing Christianity is that it can be upset by the simplest of circumstances: missing a bus and not getting to a service, or perhaps merely forgetting to say a certain prayer at a certain time; deciding that certain actions are grave sin and feeling cut off from God. These people have got on a treadmill of anxiety and as long as their God is 'he who must be pleased', they will find life a burden. A great problem for anyone trying to help is the fact that they seem unwilling to hear any message of freedom as they dig deeper into their unhappiness.

Allied to a vision of God as angry parent is the vision of hell and the devil. Many anxious people have a fear of the devil that would give Satan a power equal to God. Hell is seen as the desperate possibility of failing, and being helpless to escape from that future. Often hell and the devil become the motivation for a change in behaviour that reinforces a sense of being driven. I would not want to deny the possibility of the existence of the devil or hell, but allowing the negative to have the leading motivational role in people's lives is hardly in keeping with the message that the risen Christ has broken the power of sin and death.

Guilt and anxiety can also colour people's lives in the period of bereavement. Did I do enough for my sick parent, why wasn't I there in his or her last moments? Did I fail to love them properly? Perhaps I could have done more? Carers can quite easily get into a spiral of guilt and anxiety and never feel free to have a break to recover their energy. In the hectic times of his ministry Jesus always included time to be with his Father. Sometimes a carer can be locked into a relationship of denial and death. Mary Gordon in

Final Payments gives a good illustration of this through the novel's protagonist Isabel.

> You may wonder, as many have wondered, why I did it, why I stayed with my father all those years. Does it suggest both the monstrosity and the confusion of the issue if I say that the day Dr MacCauley told me about my father's stroke was of my whole life the day I felt most purely alive? Certainty was mine, and purity; I was encased in meaning like a crystal. It was less than three weeks after my father found me with David Lowe. Perhaps after the dull, drowning misery of those weeks, the news that brought me the possibility of a visible martyrdom was sheer relief: a grapefruit ice that cleanses the palate between courses of a heavy meal. During those weeks, we barely spoke; neither of us could invent the mechanism of forgiveness. Then my father had his stroke. In its way, it suited us to perfection.
>
> (p.10)

Isabel's father had discovered his teenage daughter's sexual relationship with a fellow student. Shortly after this episode the father has a stroke and Isabel sees caring for him as a mode of expiation. Even when her father dies, Isabel stays fixed in her life-denying mode until a chance remark brings her back to the Gospel and life. Even though Isabel comes from a most correct Catholic background, it takes a near breakdown to enable her to confront life-giving possibilities.

Another area where feelings of failure and guilt emerge is in parents' perception of their children. If teenage or adult offspring walk different paths and take up different lifestyles and beliefs, parents ask: 'Where did we go wrong?' Young adults who no longer go to Mass or have given up the faith, marriages that break down, all seem to be failures that parents must take to themselves and see as their own fault. The feeling that you have to be responsible for others, and the guilt engendered, make for intolerable burdens. The added negative element is the deepening of alienation that can follow because parents and children experience too sharp a conflict of values. Embarrassment and misunderstanding grow, often to a point of bitterness and total breakdown of relationships. There is nothing more tragic to watch than a good parent, who feels driven with anxiety about their son or daughter's lifestyle, ending up isolated and unloved because of their misplaced love.

> To remember that time is to remember a flood: the waters of my act surround me. I was drowning in that time, and drowning my father in impossible consequences. He dragged me to Confession, but I did not confess, and he never knew that I did not, and I never went again. He was silent those weeks but for his weeping, and to say, 'If you should have a child, we will keep it. We will move away somewhere and raise it.'

There is never an easy answer to situations where other people neglect or spurn what we cherish but, in the end, gentle patient presence towards others, non-threatening attitudes, are the best way. The person who can let go and let others live is freeing him- or herself to be more able to relate and, perhaps, rekindle the flame that no longer burns in the other person's life.

The area of guilt that is most oppressive and negative is sexuality. Here, reactions can often be neurotic, but too often there is a deep level of misunderstanding about what appropriate behaviour entails. The saddest form of guilt concerns divorced people. Many of those who have gone through the trauma of divorce believe that they are no longer in communion with the Church. They believe that since their marriage, their vows, are shattered, they have no right to be in the Church. 'Divorce is wrong, I am divorced, I am wrong.' Such is the reasoning based all too often on what they have heard in sermons. Marriage breakdown is a tragedy but there is no need to compound the problems so that people leave the Church because they cannot live up to its teaching. What is needed in these circumstances is generous pastoral care and support groups that can see divorcees through difficult times. It is natural to feel guilty at marriage breakdown and it is important to work on the feelings produced. However, when a woman has to seek a divorce to protect herself and her children from a brutal, cruel or inadequate person, she is using the laws of the land to protect her and her family and gain a modicum of freedom so that life can be lived in peace. At other times the breakdown comes from adultery, with one or other partner giving up on the relationship. Here, the partner who has been deserted may be left in a state of shock with a sense of bereavement – only the sense of bereavement may, perhaps, be far more difficult to cope with than if the partner had died.

The crux for a divorced person comes when they want to make a new relationship. Even though the events leading to the breakdown have been traumatic, people feel the need for companionship, for somebody significant in their lives. Often a relationship provides the healing of the person that no other form of affirmation could achieve. When we feel we have failed in some way and wonder how and why the marriage ended in the courts, to find we can reach out and be accepted by another person is life-enhancing. However, as we know, the Church sees marriage as indissoluble and cannot countenance this new relationship. After a civil divorce, a Catholic cannot enter a relationship that involves sexual intimacy without forfeiting the right to the sacraments. The reality is painful for people in this situation. They believe in the new relationship but the teaching of the Church makes them feel guilty and produces tension. Some people caught up in this predicament leave the Church – a community that seems to lack compassion in these intimate matters can hardly be the face of Christ. Many others stay in the Church and stay with the Church; these are mature people who often have worked hard at the first relationship that failed and now, perhaps, in middle age find fulfilment. It's true that the Church can offer the possibility of nullity procedure, but this is a relatively complex process and while it can be therapeutic many find it an embarrassing exercise. The plight therefore of many divorced and separated Catholics calls for a creative pastoral situation, in which they can work out whether they should be excluded from meeting Christ in the sacraments and how much they should feel that the way things are is their fault, their guilt. Certainly the way things are now does little to enable personal development.

The final group that can seem and feel to be victims

carrying guilt are homosexuals. The recent documents that have come from Rome are marked by a tone that does little to reach out a healing hand to men and women who have often suffered from the prejudices of society at large.

Prejudice and misunderstanding have marked society's view of homosexuality and the tone of some Church pronouncements has driven many gay people out of the Christian community. They feel blamed for their orientation and made to bear guilt for just being and feeling as they are. Scripture is often used and misused to justify a particular moral stance. When I was working as a university chaplain in London, a support group was set up in the Chaplaincy for gay students. One particular group of Catholics pilloried and misrepresented the initiative and refused to retract their misrepresentations. Of recent years, through contacts with the Terrence Higgins Trust and AIDS counselling groups, I have met many gay people, most of whom are gay men. What strikes me is how committed and caring towards each other these people are, and also how many of these gay people are Catholics who have become alienated from the Church. When people are trying to discover themselves they need help, not condemnation.

Sex and issues concerning relationships bring the highest incidence of guilt feelings and are also the issues that make people feel it's all too much, and they drift away from the Church. 'Drift' is the best description of what happens, a gradual feeling of alienation, of non-acceptance, a sense that nobody will address the issues with compassion. Such a reality flies in the face of the Gospel where Christ seeks out the ones who are wounded and broken. His table ministry, his sitting down with publicans and sinners, made him the one who was accessible. It was also a risky strategy and the righteous saw this availability as a fault and criticized Christ's willingness to be alongside the rejected. As disciples, can we be any different from our Master in the way we accept those around us? The reality as perceived by many people who have belonged to the Church is that they have experienced negative and even hostile reactions to their needs. They have been told they were wrong, selfish or weak. Even if people have not been told this explicitly, they often feel rejected. The absence of a caring gesture or a positive approach forces people into a wilderness not of their making.

Can and should this paradoxical situation be allowed to continue? Why have we as a community become known as an anxious and too often guilt-ridden tribe? Many might feel that this is a harsh perception and a too easily applied stereotype. But this perception is based in a reality. There is a need to see why things are the way they are and to find ways of enabling the Gospel message of freedom to be a reality and a source of hope once again.

2

□

A style of teaching

□

Where does this paradox come from, that people who should be freed and enabled by the Gospel are in fact driven, guilt-ridden and anxious? In the first place it originates, I believe, in a style of teaching that gives people too much too quickly and relies on a negative tone. David Lodge, in *How Far Can You Go?*, paints an accurate picture of what is involved:

Before we go any further it would probably be a good idea to explain the metaphysic or world-picture these young people had acquired from their Catholic upbringing and education. Up there was Heaven; down there was Hell. The name of the game was Salvation, the object to get to Heaven and avoid Hell. It was like Snakes and Ladders: sin sent you plummeting down towards the Pit; the sacraments, good deeds, acts of self-mortification, enabled you to climb back towards the light. Everything you did or thought was subject to spiritual accounting. It was either good, bad or indifferent. Those who succeeded in the game eliminated the bad and converted as much of the indifferent as possible for the good. Progress towards Heaven was full of such pitfalls. On the whole, a safe rule of thumb was that anything you positively disliked doing was probably good, and anything you liked doing enormously was probably bad, or potentially bad – an 'occasion of sins'.

There were two types of sin, venial and mortal.

Venial sins were little sins which only slightly retarded
your progress across the board. Mortal sins were huge
snakes that sent you slithering back to square one,
because if you died in a state of mortal sin, you went to
Hell. If, however, you confessed your sins and received
absolution through the sacrament of Penance, you
shot up the ladder of grace to your original position
on the board, though carrying a penalty − a certain
amount of punishment awaiting you in the next world.
For few Catholics expected that they would have
reached the heavenly finishing line by the time they
died. Only saints would be in that happy position, and
to consider yourself a saint was a sure sign that you
weren't one: there was a snake called Presumption that
was just as fatal as the one called Despair. (It really
was a most ingenious game.) No, the vast majority of
Catholics expected to spend a certain amount of time
in Purgatory first.

(Penguin edition (London, 1988), pp. 6−7)

Lodge's sketch shows us individuals struggling to overcome
an obstacle course set up by an almost malign power. There
is no room for a God who invites people into a loving
relationship, but rather there is the pitfall of sin. Basically
everyone seems to be in a 'no win' situation, and salvation
seems to be almost a matter of chance, success in the lottery
of life. There is of course an element of caricature in Lodge's
description but it is nonetheless based on real experience. He
grew up in the 1950s and his experience would be typical of
that of most adults in the Church today. Even if they have
heard a more sensitive proclamation of the message based
on Vatican II, the deep psychological formation has already
taken place and the process of learning anew is difficult. It
takes time, it needs a good guide and perhaps such help
has not been accessible for the majority of people. The
consequences of this are that despite Vatican II, despite
so much work for renewal, we must recognize that David
Lodge's affectionate caricature is still reflecting attitudes
that are alive and influential. Joy, pleasure and happiness
are elements of life that remain suspect: what matters more
is correct behaviour.

Earlier on, the tone of teaching was described as negative. This is a factor that is as important as the content of what is taught. Style, tone and form are all as influential as content. The tone of voice changes or nuances meaning and, even if a renewed theology is presented, when the style of teaching has not changed then little in the way of renewal has been achieved.

In recent times the greatest effort, especially in English-speaking countries, in teaching Christianity has been concentrated in our schools or parishes. The aim of so much of this work has been to produce good Catholics. Behind such an aim there is an anxiety that if we do not get as much as possible taught during childhood and teenage years then 'we have failed'. Priests and teachers have been under enormous pressure to succeed and catechetical programmes and RE syllabuses have been tested against a success-by-numbers mind-set. The result is a cry going up that teenagers nowadays do not go to Mass, whereas in the days of cut-and-dried teaching they did. Few people ask the question: is it right to expect every sixteen-year-old to be ready to make an act of faith in God? Can a teenager understand in the core of their being how God yearns to be their lover? Is there a need to experience what it means to live and love before we reach out to the transcendent?

The crux of the matter is a hidden agenda in our religious education. We find ourselves transferring to the work of religious and personal development the mentality of success and failure that we associate with public examination results. When I was at school we even used to have, on Monday, a register of who had attended Mass and who had missed Mass. Today we would not ask such questions but we still privately make a count of those who 'practise'. It means that religious formation is governed by external criteria like English or physics. The consequence of all this for the Catholic community is a failure in catechesis and renewal. Older people are still moulded in a basically pessimistic vision, while the young have no real opportunity to hear the Gospel at the time they are finding or trying to find meaning in life.

We need to change our attitudes and to find out what lies behind the anxious and driven mind-set. Going back to our text from Lodge, we see the Catholic world-view dominated by sin and a sense that we are basically incapable of doing good. Human nature must be flawed and, even if grace saves us from terminal disaster, we are never quite out of the wood. There will always be some penalty to pay because of the offences we have committed.

The only way forward must be to look at the basics of Christian teaching about the human condition and ask whether they have helped or hindered a full human development.

When Jesus proclaimed the Good News he called people to live that Good News, and so the New Testament describes communities of disciples, assemblies of people who saw holiness as their ambition. But they are people who have been called to holiness by listening to Jesus and then committing themselves to his message. The notion of a people chosen by God is basic. A community is envisaged, the ones Jesus saved are the lost and despised that he brings into the warmth of the community. He came to bring life to the sinner so that he or she could once again experience the joy of the family and join in the feast of life. One of the significant aspects of Jesus' work was his table ministry – the way he was able to sit down to meals with the virtuous and the sinner, the Pharisee and the prostitute. People instinctively felt at ease and they were able to come out of their isolation and into life once more. Jesus helped people feel good and the way forward for them was to accept their need of healing. The only barrier to change was a misplaced individualism, a pride.

People today rarely feel they belong. Communities exist but are not bonded by values or some shared spirit. Sometimes fear bonds a community. Inner-city communities are often so terrorized by criminals that a bizarre solidarity emerges, born of the fear of those who control them. Often the big drug barons so terrify people that even when murders occur, people are too frightened to speak out or break ranks. Other communities are bonded by respectability. The 'neighbourhood watch' stickers can stand for preservation of property, keeping out the stranger and perhaps keeping a curious eye on what our unknown neighbour could be up to. The lonely individual who populates our society, the one who is on their own, is a product of modern individualism. This individualism affects Christian thinking too, and there are those who see the Church as a community of individuals who have been saved.

Jesus spoke to the whole person and wanted to include the whole person in the community. He healed the illness and forgave the sin and excluded nobody. To be human was to be open to a relationship with the Father, and all were able to be sons and daughters. All of us had been chosen and were to be God's work of art. Yet within a few generations of Jesus, the work of art was being described as *massa damnata*, a condemned people. The human race had suffered some primeval catastrophe and the images of sin, the Fall and hell began to dominate:

> Of Man's first disobedience, and the fruit
> of that forbidden tree, whose mortal taste
> brought death into the world, and all our woe,
> with loss of Eden ... (Opening of *Paradise Lost*)

Graham Greene reflects a contemporary sense of this fallen desolate world when he writes of his perception of religion and belief. 'And so faith came to one ... something associated with violence, cruelty, evil across the way. One began to believe in heaven because one believed in hell. It remained something one associated with misery, violence, evil' (*The Lawless Roads*, pp. 14, 15). In his essay 'The Lost Childhood' he is even more extreme: 'But the pattern was already there – perfect evil walking the world where perfect good can never walk again' (*Collected Essays*, p. 17). The poem 'Germinal' by AE is perhaps even more stark:

> In ancient shadows and twilights
> Where childhood had strayed
> The world's great sorrows were born
> And its heroes were made
> In the lost boyhood of Judas
> Jesus was betrayed.

Where does this dark shadow vision come from, which overlays Christianity with a sense of sin, while virtue seems to be in abeyance? The Christian faith should be based on the conviction that God has recreated us in the image of

Christ and so lives of thoroughgoing integrity are possible. The perceived reality is that the old Adam rather than the Christ is in the foreground.

More and more theologians are of the opinion that the way the doctrine of original sin has been presented is at the root of so many negative attitudes that prevail among Christians. We have to ask, was there a primeval calamity, was there a specific sin, and must we with Augustine believe that there is a predisposition in human nature to evil?

The doctrine of original sin received its formulation at the hands of St Augustine as he disputed with the British monk, Pelagius. In fact it was Augustine who first used the phrase 'original sin' to describe the human condition as he envisaged it. Most writers agree that Augustine's vision of life, of human nature, was clouded by pessimism and strongly influenced by shame at his own behaviour as a young man. The society in which Augustine lived was in a state of transition as the Roman Empire crumbled and the Germanic tribes began to overrun the Mediterranean countries. This too fuelled his pessimism.

The sweep and range of Augustine's teaching is beyond doubt, and he was the great authority that formed the medieval mind. However, in his moral teaching there is a darkness that is almost a moral pessimism. But it is also important to remember that Augustine's teachings were used by others down the centuries. What was powerful rhetoric from the mouth of Augustine was often reduced to textbook dryness by those who quarried his work in later times. The medieval world with its wars and plagues, the sudden visitations of death, found an explanation for such darkness and disaster in Augustine's vision of human frailty and sin. Augustine, a great, even sublime man, time and again in his writings speaks of human beings with melancholy, disgust and harshness, because the fall from God's grace in Adam has made them weak and sinful.

Augustine saw the original sin of Adam as the beginning of disorder and chaos. The pride behind the sin caused a rift with God and produced the divided self. The disorder now reverberates through history. The consequence of that first disobedience is a great sadness, with human nature now damaged and that same nature now marked by lust and lack of insight. In *The City of God*, Augustine actually says 'The human race is then *massa damnata* (a condemned people)'. Later on in the *Enchiridion* he writes even more dramatically:

This therefore was the case: the damned mass of the whole race was lying, was indeed wallowing, in evils, being tossed from evils to evils and, being joined to the faction of those angels who had sinned, was paying the most frightful penalty of its wicked disloyalty.

Augustine's pessimism about human nature was rooted in his personal experience. When he was a young intellectual he had joined the Manichees. They saw evil as a force fighting good, way beyond human power and involvement. Later, in Milan, he was drawn to Neoplatonism, which helped him to value virtue from an intellectual standpoint, but he could not give up his sinful way of life. He did in the end have a conversion experience and what was impossible, a remote ideal, was now within his grasp. Grace made the impossible possible, but he could not forget the reality of evil. For Augustine the explanation was the flawed nature that we have inherited from Adam. It was this position that angered Pelagius the Celtic monk, and led to a ferocious theological controversy which made Augustine express his opinions about the human condition in a most dramatic and forceful way. It is the heat of these debates that had so much influence on the Church's teaching about human nature and human relationship with God.

Augustine's vision was that we all have a solidarity with Adam's sin by our very nature. Though we are regenerated by grace in baptism we still remain wounded. There is still in us a predisposition to evil which he called concupiscence and in this we have a solidarity with the first humans, Adam and Eve, who by their pride fell from God's favour.

'For we were all that one man Adam when we were that one man who fell into sin ... Not yet had the particular form been created and apportioned to us in which we were individually to live but there was a seminal nature from which we were to be propagated' (*The City of God*). This language passed into traditional teaching and was formalized in the decrees in which the Council of Trent affirms that the guilt of original sin is remitted at baptism but also says: 'The Holy Council knows and professes that concupiscence or the inclination to sin remains in the baptized − since it is left for us to wrestle with it.'

Sin and concupiscence have another dimension in the teaching of Augustine. The young Augustine had been dominated by his sexual urges and the consequent dissipation. This domination of the body humiliated the intellectual side of him and he saw this as the law and life of sin alive in his body. On the one hand these bodily desires made him aware of the results of original sin and on the other hand intercourse seemed like the channel for transmitting sin. Sexual intercourse took on a negative meaning and could only be good when it was specifically meant to be an act of procreation. Sexual activity was so overpowering for the person that it could only be right if a child was envisaged. Other appetites of the body could be exercised, because they were easier to control. Wine and food were not so dangerous because they could often go along with philosophical conversation. Sexual activity was far too divorced from the mind or the spirit. In the end, for Augustine, only a well-ordered love of God mattered. But where in all this was there a positive vision of women? Augustine tended to see them as passive receptacles who were incapable of mental stimulus. It would seem that women were merely objects of desire, there to procreate but incapable of providing man with friendship; that, along with mental stimulus, could only be found in another man.

In all this we see Augustine concentrating on human weaknesses, seeing humans as sinners constantly in need of help. There was no vision of human beings called to perfection, or capable of developing strengths or virtues. It was his vision that was to dominate the Middle Ages and inspire the Reformers and be the driving force of moral theology and an awareness of humanity right up to our own age. For the best part of 1,500 years, the mood of Augustine has been dominant in moral theology in the West. But what Augustine said needs to be balanced by other voices because no one teacher can ever pronounce the final word about the way we relate to God and God relates to us. We must remember that there was a Christian vision before Augustine and there are other insights that can contribute to another vision.

This tradition leaves us with a lack of self-worth, a feeling that in our moral behaviour and especially in sexual morality we will fail because we are flawed. It seems that there is an inevitable bias towards failure.

The presence of evil is never so powerful either in our personal life or in the world around us as to prevent us from longing and yearning for God in the depths of our being. However, because we believe we are flawed, we do not know how to handle our yearning for fulfilment and we turn to possessions, to frenetic relationships, to anything that will mask the hurt and the need; in that process we intensify the pain and feel more and more unhappy about who and how we are. We seem to be in a 'Catch-22' situation; we are as we are because of original sin and, because of what it has done to our nature, we can only remain as we are. It is this mind-set that in the end makes the sin of Adam feel more powerful and effective in our lives than the saving work of Jesus. Jesus came to be the truth that sets us free, he has taken on human nature to show its goodness because it is the image of God. He also took on himself the sin of the world so that his death could be life-giving and a source of regeneration for all humanity. God wants us to know that we can be recreated in the image of his Son and that lives of deep human integrity are possible. God is a God of forgiveness who heals, not a power of wrath and vindictiveness.

Is it possible to express the doctrine of original sin in such a way that it does not overwhelm us with negative consequences? At the heart of Christian teaching is the saving work of Christ which came from his loving obedience to the Father. This offers to all the saving grace of God which has total effectiveness. The obedience of Christ is in contrast to all other responses, and in the writings of Paul it is set in powerful contrast to the disobedience of Adam. Paul contrasts Christ and Adam and shows that in Christ all is made new and a totally new path is open to humanity.

The factor that has to be accounted for is the way good and evil are found in human behaviour. Are we created with a tendency to evil or is it part of our social situation, our history? Paul speaks of the divided self: 'For I do not do the thing I want but the thing I hate' (Romans 7:15).

We need to look at creation and what critical study of the Bible has to tell us about the early chapters of Genesis. The teaching about creation and original sin is closely linked. We need to understand that God created the world but he also needed to heal it, and that human beings experience rebellion against God as well as love of God. This situation is a permanent part of being human.

In the story of the Fall the writers of Genesis are trying to answer the question 'Why is there such a mixture of good and evil in individuals and society?' People and societies are a bewildering mixture of good and evil. A man can be a tender parent and yet in his professional life be ruthless to protect his interests. An artist can create the sublime and yet have a chaotic sexual life. The biblical writers tell us that in our origins we got ourselves into a state of estrangement by trying to be like God, by overreaching pride, and this estrangement is now at the root of our divided self. In the story, Adam and Eve, by their reactions of blaming others, show the unwillingness to take responsibility so engrained in society where people blame others for their actions. What the story tells us is that evil came through a historical situation, that evil is not part of creation.

It is vital to make this point because creation is God's work and, as God's goodness cannot create anything but good, evil must have its origins since creation, in history. It is something that has happened to the good, a distortion of reality that comes from the misuse of intelligence and freedom.

Genesis tells us that God is creator, but it does not say exactly how creation took place. In affirming God's creative work, it frees those who hear the story from fears about nature, and also points out that men and women have a tremendous responsibility for the creation in which they live. They are an integral part of the creative work but because of their God-given ability to relate they stand at a crossroads between the planet and God.

Exactly how God created is not part of the Bible story but it is part of the story of human perception and intelligence.

Gradually we have come to accept that the theory of evolution tells us something about how the universe moved from its first existence to our present moment in history. Creation is energy suffused in matter, as Einstein and the quantum theory tell us. Perhaps the process of evolution of our universe is at its half-way stage. What we also know is the unity of creation: mineral, animal, vegetable are all part of the same complex, the same stuff – we are all carbon-based reality.

The evolutionary view of creation has important qualifications for the human species and, as a consequence, for our understanding of original sin, and good and evil. For so long the human race was viewed as separate from the rest of creation, and the link between the animate, the inanimate and the human race was lost. Our roots in our environment were lost and the fact we are both animal and yet have a yearning for the spiritual has been ignored by a one-sided stress on the spiritual. At some point in history, the human emerged and, while physical evolution is probably complete for our species, we are still developing. It is this evolving being who is open to God's saving plan, not a creature who was once in some original state of perfection; we need not always be looking back, but we can understand the consequences of our origins and of the needs that accompany the development of our species. When human beings emerged, the factors that made them different included the ability to communicate, to possess self-awareness and to realize that death was part of existence. Self-awareness was the crucial element as it made human beings aware of the choices they could make as they interacted. Before humans achieved self-awareness, the primates were at peace, living by their instincts. If they were attacked they would fight or flee according to circumstances; food kept hunger at bay, so if there were no external threats and the environment was friendly, they were at peace. However, once self- and herd-preservation were no longer the only motives of behaviour, then consciousness would not allow us to rest in the lesser peace of the irrational animal. Instincts and drives had to be shaped and directed. There was the need to face up to our basic instincts and feelings and make them part of the whole.

The new awareness could be used for creative and caring behaviour or it could be the dynamism for cruelty and pain. Humankind has its monuments, both to the ruins of the battlefield and to the domestic landscape that shows harmonious and peaceful existence.

Bringing reason and instinct into harmony is the great project for the human race, so that we may become truly human. At the moment we are still working at discerning what it is to be human, how we integrate the elements of our personality. We cannot succeed if we deny the conflict within us, and refuse to acknowledge our instinctual feelings and drives. This happens all too often when, having made a mistake, we run away rather than face up to the result: for example, drivers who flee from the scene of an accident. We feel angry and wonder why we have panicked, perhaps even deny the fear. But we have learnt from modern behavioural science to acknowledge and face our instinctual feelings and drives. Our culture, which has so often rejoiced in the rational, must accept the shadow, or the non-rational. Energies denied are destructive; recognized and harnessed, they become sources of energy.

It is in this context that we recognize the need to be redeemed. We have both the help and the model to enable us to strive towards full humanity, in the life of Jesus. Jesus shows us the possibility of being human and being without sin. In Jesus we see feelings expressed, not denied, yet all achieved appropriately. John Cleese once observed that though he was not a Christian, he always admired the way Jesus could express the deepest feeling and then move on to the next part of his life, exhibiting the appropriate reaction. Paul expressed it beautifully in Ephesians when he said we are 'God's work of art'. Given the empowerment of grace, so much more can be achieved than we ever imagined. Grace enables us to accept and transform our primal emotions.

This evolutionary view of life which sees us with God's help becoming more fully human means that we do not have to think that we should be perfect straight away. When we have impossible standards we are bound to fail and it is too easy to translate that happening into the feeling 'I am a failure'. If I am a failure, I am not good, so there must be a flaw within me that is impossible to eradicate.

It's all too easy to go from that sense of failure to saying it's hopeless, and to begin to drift away from any attempt to be open to God. We begin to believe we are rejected, and that is the great untruth that has brought untold misery to all too many. No, we are constantly striving to discover how we can realize the humanity revealed by Jesus and we know that as long as we strive we will be helped. The times when our actions lack harmony give us insight into where we need God's grace: our weakness becomes our strength. Dorothee Soelle makes the beautiful comment 'I have noticed that people with faith all walk with a limp'. The wounds of our weakness show how we come to closeness with God.

An important element in the process of becoming human is our use of conscience. There are many neat definitions of conscience that would reduce it to a faculty and in this way only continue the fragmentation of the human person. It is perhaps best to see conscience as the moral consciousness or awareness of a person. It is this particular person making choices as she or he is, with all the experiences, bias and baggage that make up that person. When a person makes a choice there are many complex elements coming together. There is the need to understand the situation, make a judgement and come to terms with the feelings aroused. Also there is the role of imagination as we wonder about the outcome of our behaviour. How I judge, how I choose, depends on the influences that I allow to form me. If I live or try to live by Gospel values then I will want to grow in wisdom and grace. I will want to search for truth and overcome bias and so I will look for authentic ways of realizing my choices. However, even if I look to Gospel values or feel at ease with the teaching of the Church as a guide, there will still be problematic factors. First, there will be bias which comes from my upbringing. I am white, middle-aged, male and educated in the liberal university tradition; how far will that prevent me from being open or humble in spirit? Will I be biased against women, black people or the young? Again my perception of reality is bound to be limited and, added to that, I am unconsciously selective. In the end we have to fall back on simple standards such as 'Would I like somebody to do this to me?' or 'Am I loving my neighbour as myself?'

The development of our conscience is a crucial part of our becoming fully human. Overcoming bias means challenging perceptions and reactions that are too facile or stereotypical. This is why imagination is crucial in forming conscience, and literature, theatre, cinema, all stimulate our imagination and help overcome bias. Comedy is one of the great enablers as, by its stark contrasts, it propels us out of convention into change. Watching a character in a novel can enable us to recognize traits that are alive and well in us. The theatre with its immediacy can demonstrate the consequences of that pride which refuses compromise. History too is a teacher as we see how burying conscience, not bothering to examine matters, has allowed others to commit horrendous crimes. Dictators often come to power on the back of indifference and subservience and commit their crimes because too many lack conviction and the courage to voice their feelings.

A conscience, then, that is directed not only to being correct or merely observing the law will enable us to grow as people. It will not be something negative, merely saying this is wrong, but it will enable us into the positive, into virtuous growth. It will make us the good tree, bringing forth the fruits of love, truth, justice and mercy.

Conscience is a crucial element in the process of attaining humanity. While we know the value of law and obedience we can learn also to own our decisions and feel at ease with what we do. In recent years we have seen the results of uncritical obedience where people have not tested orders against higher values. The prophetic element in Christianity always challenges us to move on to new things, and new information can cause us to question what has been acceptable in the past. Here we come to questions like war and social justice, which will deserve to be treated in a later chapter.

The vision then of humanity as a goal to be reached, both by the human race as a whole and by each individual journeying through life does, I think, both address the reality called original sin and accept the presence of evil. It does, however, give us a much greater sense of hope and also allows us to see the healing and fulfilling role of grace. It shows us human life as part of an evolving process of creation, and in that process redemption has a clear place. It challenges us to see ourselves as a whole and to realize that the whole person is achieved through redemption − grace is the integrating factor that enables the animal and the angel to be at ease together. When we are healed and whole we have a marvellous potential for growth.

Pope John XXIII and Pope Paul VI reminded us that the dogmas − the basic teaching of faith − can never change, but they also made it clear that the expression of such dogmas was open to new formulations. Anything basic in faith can never be completely described by one formulation and it is clear that Augustine's approach to original sin, and the style of teaching flowing from it, have not been speaking to our age. The call to holiness, our need of redemption, the consequences of our finiteness − these are all unchanging realities, but how we grapple with their meaning for our lives is a challenge for every age.

Certainly the legacy of this style of teaching has left many of our generation adrift, lonely and feeling confused and guilty. It is at variance with the vision that we as persons can grow, and it does not seem to value the human. We can have the feeling that this is something unjust and imposed on us. This feeling of injustice is compounded by the fact that Augustine would seem to say that our sexuality and its expression is inextricably bound with original sin and its consequences. Most people would feel that this style of teaching does little to help them achieve healthy and whole development as persons.

At the end of the twentieth century we need a more positive approach; otherwise our society will have no vision and end up as a mere collection of lonely individuals with no sense of a meaning in their lives. The novels of Kingsley Amis and his son Martin in their various ways show this bleakness. Kingsley Amis deals with ageing in his two novels *Ending Up* and *The Old Devils*. In *Ending Up*, a group of unattractive elderly folk live together, drawn into a sort of community by a series of accidents. In old age they have lost their attractiveness and as a result they prey on one another with malicious intent. A misplaced practical joke starts off a chain of events that ends up with all of them dying, and because of their irrelevance they are never missed. *The Old Devils* charts a landscape of bleak late middle age where relationships and academic promise have crumbled and drink has become the only solace. Kingsley Amis charts his worlds with a grim humour, but even he would wish for something other than the bleakness he portrays. He would hope that someone could reawaken a sense of belief, even though he might still disagree with it.

3

□

Free for all

□

In the novel *The Bonfire of the Vanities*, a mock epic of New York life in the 1980s, Tom Wolfe writes of the Masters of the Universe − bond dealers, a new breed spawned by the aftermath of the Vietnam War and the rise of oil prices in the 1970s. Sherman McCoy, the anti-hero of the book, a successful dealer, dreams of making more money to cushion his already elaborate lifestyle.

The only real problem was the complexity of the thing.
It took big sophisticated investors to understand it . . .
you had to have a track record. You had to have
talent − genius − mastery of the universe − like
Sherman McCoy. The deal would bring Pierce and
Pierce $6 million − Sherman's share would come to
$1.75 million. With that he intended to pay off the
horrendous $1.8 million personal loan he had taken out
to buy the apartment.
As Sherman dialled and waited for Bernard Levy to
come on the line, the rousing sound of the greed storm
closed in about him once again.

(Picador edition (1990), pp. 76−7)

Later in the novel, just before his downfall, Sherman and his city are portrayed in all their power:

There it was, the Rome, the Paris, the London of
the twentieth century, the city of ambition, the dense
magnetic rock, the irresistible destination of all those

33

who insist on being where it's happening – and he
was among the victors. He lived on Park Avenue. The
street of dreams. He worked on Wall Street, fifty floors
up, for the legendary Pierce and Pierce, overlooking
the world! He was at the wheel of a $48,000 roadster
with one of the most beautiful women in New York –
a frisky young animal. He was of that breed whose
natural destiny it was to have what they wanted.

(Ibid., p. 91)

Sherman McCoy epitomizes how people see the world of
finance today. True, he is a character in a novel, but he is a
perception of the storyteller, an observer of life. Sherman is
an icon of success and he is quite unashamedly a product of
a culture of greed. He will have what he wants and the only
cost he knows is ultimately on a balance sheet. Sherman is
self-styled master of the universe, a title he can claim because
with the help of electronic systems the world is his village,
and he seems with the help of information technology to
be totally in charge. However, Sherman is not meant to be
taken for real, he is meant to be a terrible warning of the
consequences of greed as motivation for doing business.

Sherman stands for those who define themselves by what
they have. The danger is that such a way of life erodes
the real person and means that greed dominates at the
expense of all that can make us fully human. What the
individual can get is what matters; the group is only
useful when it is a means to ensuring that the individual
is successful. Community and what is happening to other
people just does not figure. Sherman has made millions but
his money has come through dealing in such a negative
way that his seeming success will contain the seeds of his
undoing. A former chairman of the Stock Exchange, Sir
Nicholas Goodison, commented in an interview that greed
was always an unsatisfactory motive in finance. Some people
would go for the best deal with no risks for themselves, but
sound business did not listen to greed. For Sir Nicholas, no
one was in business just for the bottom-line profit; profit
was a resource that should serve the whole community.

Here then are two pictures of the world of commerce and
finance where many people spend most of their working

lives. It is a world fraught with dilemmas and yet one where the voice of Christianity can be blocked out. If people have not found a coherent message for their personal lives, how can they look to the institutional Church for guidance in the cut and thrust of dealing, of take-over bids and often of just trying to survive in a cold economic climate?

More and more people in the business world are asking who is responsible? Can a company be guilty? Where does accountability lie? What becomes more and more apparent is the sense of groups operating inside a closed world with no thought of the consequences of their action. Currency speculation is one activity that has devastating effects. When a country's currency becomes the target of speculators for whatever reason then thousands of ordinary people suffer the consequences of the resulting devaluation. A rumour is picked up on the Hong Kong market and, by the time Wall Street closes, a nation's economy is in ruins. The electronic world transmits and circulates the news so that pounds, punts and lire are unleashed on the market in a dizzying spiral of devaluation. The only people to gain are currency speculators. In September 1992, when the pound was forced out of the ERM, one such speculator made over 2,000 million dollars but this man, George Soros, has shown he has a human face, because he has used a large slice of his profits to alleviate suffering in former Yugoslavia.

It is in this fast-moving complex world of modern business that questions about guilt, responsibility and business ethics arise. It is all too easy to show a judgemental attitude against the world of commerce. The Church can adopt an attitude that could seem as negative as its approach to personal morality, or it could seek to be a source that enables the men and women involved in decision-making in business to feel they have some sort of map to help them forward.

Business enterprises need to make a profit if they are to survive and, in an increasingly competitive world, profit margins can vanish. Therefore, management has to be shrewd and realistic, without resorting to strategems that flout the law. There are obvious cases where companies have overstepped the mark. The Guinness case saw eagerness to outdo a rival bid leading to practices that amounted to fraud. British Airways and Virgin Atlantic fought to gain a market share and it would seem that British Airways stooped to tactics that were far from fair. There are notable examples of mismanagement such as the Maxwell empire and the BCCI affair. These cases all made headlines, but they can hardly be said to represent the reality of the business world. On both sides of the Atlantic there is great concern about the ethics of business and any business enterprise that wants to flourish needs to be firmly rooted in sound practice.

The questions that need to be asked in the world of business and commerce hinge on who takes responsibility and, if there is guilt, who has to say 'I was at fault', 'We made a mistake'. Decisions taken at senior management levels can seem feasible and clear but at the point of delivery there can be problems. So a crucial element in good practice is good communication. If a company delivering a service agrees to fulfil its obligations under certain time constraints it is often the local manager who has to say he is happy with the situation. However, if he is saving time at the expense of safety, then this information has to be communicated upwards. Sometimes organizations lack good avenues of communication or, again, the person at the point of delivery wants to impress those above and is tempted to take risks. An example could be in the field of road haulage where short cuts could be made in servicing trucks or asking a driver to work one shift too many. It is obvious that if the contract is based on tight margins then tight controls will be in place, and yet good management must analyse right down the line to see if good working practices are respected. Given this sort of procedure, those concerned with the project have to listen to each other with great honesty. The danger can be to say 'Yes, it is possible', because we want to impress, we want to please. A junior manager can say yes to his superior and then pressurize a driver, an engineer, a fitter. Management structures should not leave individuals in positions where they are put under pressure to perform and then have to take responsibility for anything that goes wrong. Responsibility must be shared.

High standards or responsibility and good training make for an efficient organization and also one that is less likely to indulge in dubious or dangerous practices. It means that people know where they stand and what is realistically expected of them. The culture of blaming rather than owning cannot flourish where a team of responsible individuals is in place.

When a company is well run it regards its human resources as its greatest asset and respects their input. In a good climate employees feel empowered and believe they have the possibility of changing or challenging what they feel uncomfortable about. In that climate the chance of accidents or anything hurtful to the customer or the consumer is slight. The problem lies with companies that are less than professional or who have failed to see the complexity of society. This happens when senior management have not thought things out or created a climate for listening. The problem for employees who blow the whistle on dubious practices is that they risk losing their job. An enterprise fuelled by greed will not value its human resources.

The same kind of issues arise in relation to the arms trade, and for all involved in military affairs. So how can anyone, Christian or not, have a commitment to standards and avoid being sucked into the machine of money, investment or war? All these negative elements seem to come from the same source that Jesus named in the Gospel, the father of lies (John 8:44) – the great myth which would say that life has to be shaped this way, there is no alternative.

The most successful companies would appear to be the most ethical, those who see a longer time-scale than a quick profit. They operate on a vision of building relationships based on trust. Companies that have a sense of responsibility also operate on a willingness to be accountable, and if a product or procedure is criticized they are willing to dialogue. This can result in a change of practice or dropping a product.

Shareholders and consumers can make their voices heard and not feel powerless or vaguely guilty about the way things are. In our society individuals can form pressure groups to effect change and can challenge gross inequalities.

When it comes to challenging the product, we do have the possibility of exercising personal choice. Agonizing achieves very little, but making decisions about what we buy can have cumulative results. Recycling projects make good sense on every level and we are the people that ensure the projects' success. Likewise an irrelevant product will die the death if we walk past it on the supermarket shelf, and we may decide not to eat exotic fruit or vegetables from the Third World when we know that they are grown at the cost of malnutrition back in the country of origin.

The world of business, the market-place, is where a country earns its living. Profit is important, but what is crucial is the way money is made, and that this is not at the cost of individuals either losing their integrity or being exploited. We need a sound economy so that we can all develop and all feel we have some share in society. The soundness depends on everyone at every level being willing to take responsibility for what happens. The danger can be feeling powerless or not believing we have the power. Perhaps the Church's role in this field should become one that calls people to a sense of their capacity to influence events in the public domain rather than just to emphasize private morality.

There is a growing awareness that there is a need for an ethic. The various approaches to public and business life whether free-for-all or corporate systems all seem to fail the vulnerable and lack respect for the individual. Untrammelled freedom does not bring universal benefits but in the end causes the opposite, a trickle up of wealth. A rigid state control has the effect of stifling initiative and ends up with a grey bureaucracy or Marxist state. The most hopeful way forward is to combine encouragement for individual freedom and initiative with a care by the state for the overall good. The mixed economy operates not in a vacuum but in a world where solidarity, global interdependence, is the reality.

I believe that the Judaeo-Christian tradition does give a basis for a social, political and economic ethic. It is a tradition that sees justice as a foundation for how people can live in such a way that they realize their God-given dignity. The prophets stress a society where justice reigns. Their vision of the messianic society is one of harmony. The Old Testament shows an opposition between the kingly mentality and the prophetic consciousness. The kings want to interpret the mind of God to the people to their own advantage so that religion becomes the respectable cloak

for their power politics. The result of Israel's involvement
in power politics is national disaster and, at the restoration
of the people from exile, the prophet in the 'book on
consolation' of Isaiah marks the way forward by challenging
them to create a community of justice and sharing:

> If you do away with the yoke,
> the clenched fist, the wicked word,
> if you give your bread to the hungry,
> and relief to the oppressed,
> your light will rise in the darkness,
> and your shadows become like noon.
>
> (Isaiah 58:9 – 10)

Jesus took his agenda from the prophets and, in the synagogue at Nazareth (Luke 4), he announces he has come to
'bring sight to the blind and freedom for prisoners'. His
Kingdom, the reign of his Father, will come, and a time of
peace, because truth and justice flourish and life is expressed
mercifully. In his epistle James reminds us that true religion
is to come to the aid of the widow and the oppressed, and
the sin that cries to heaven is defrauding the worker of
his wages.

The prophetic tradition which Jesus fulfils seeks to create
a situation where men and women can realize their dignity
and be open to God. Full humanity is the goal and anything
less is unsatisfactory. I believe that this prophetic tradition
is being articulated in the twentieth century by the Church's
social teaching, which does offer a vision of how we can live
in the complex world that is ours. Beginning with Pope Leo
XIII's letter on social issues in 1891, *Rerum Novarum,* and
down to our own day, the Catholic community has looked
at the world of business, politics and economics and asked
how human dignity, solidarity and the common good can be
best served.

The American bishops among others articulated their
stance on the economy after wide-ranging consultation:

> Private property does not constitute for anyone an
> absolute or unconditional right. No one is justified in
> keeping for his (or her) exclusive use what he (or she)
> does not need, when others lack necessities ...

The ... church opposes all statist and totalitarian economic approaches to socio-economic questions. Social life is richer than governmental power can encompass. All groups that compose society have responsibilities to respond to the demands of justice ...

For this reason ... the teachings of the Church insist that government has a moral function: protecting human rights and securing basic justice for all members of the commonwealth.

(Economic Justice for All: Pastoral Letter on Catholic Teaching and the US Economy (1986), nos 115, 121, 122)

Another aspect of Catholic social teaching is subsidiarity, whereby a higher authority only takes on tasks in society that cannot be properly carried out at the local level. The state or the corporation should not quash initiative but conversely it should not ignore problems that are beyond the group at local level. So there should be no undue interference from on high and, conversely, no deaf ear when help is needed. This approach can be creative in political, social and economic affairs.

The indiscriminate use of freedom is seen as destructive in the Catholic tradition: freedom has to look to a social order. We are not a group of individuals existing without responsibilities to each other and especially to the vulnerable. Freedom taken to extremes can mean misery for many and, when freedom means an indiscriminate use of the planet's resources, then it means we have ceased to share in the Creator's freedom – freedom linked to responsibility. We are not meant to exploit the earth but to hold it in stewardship for God, in partnership, and one day we are meant to restore creation to God. The fact that modern science and technology have given us such power over the planet does not give us licence to destroy or plunder it. The German bishops make the point in a declaration published in 1980:

The world is God's gift to humanity, given to humanity to pass on. Man therefore has responsibility for the generations that come after him. In this way the creation becomes an inheritance which each generation owes to the one that comes after it and which it cannot

consume away or burden with intolerable mortgages ...
We are not creators, but the created. To seek to be
lords over all, as God is, is the origin of sin. We
cannot start from nothing to attain our desires and
wishes without limit. For us freedom means accepting
that freedom and using it with the conditions attached
to it. The Creator gives us a share in his creative
freedom. We must have the courage to develop this.
That presupposes the courage to accept and receive it as
the gift of God. There is a spirituality in the Christian
relationship to the world that arises from the basic
slogan: 'Acceptance and response'.
(German Bishops' Conference. Declaration on
Environmental Questions and Energy Supplies,
  'The Future of Creation − Future of Mankind' (1980))

Finally, does the Church bless war or has its vision
evolved? Ever since Augustine, the just war theory has
prevailed in Western Christianity. However, in the early
Church, killing was seen as a grave sin and that meant all
forms of killing, even in war. The early Christians chose to
refuse to be part of the Roman military machine and this
became a reason for their persecution. From the time of
Constantine onwards, Church and state began to collaborate
and the just war became the order of the day. The present
Pope has stated that war should no longer be on the agenda
of humanity and that we should be building the cathedral of
peace. When Stanley Kubrick translated Anthony Burgess's
novel *A Clockwork Orange* into a film he withdrew it
because of the effect of its violence. The violent, mindless
society he visualized is an imaging of how far we can go.
That is why the counter-culture of Christianity is worth
heeding and being invested with energy and imagination so
that it can be realized.

4

□

Guilty of being a woman

□

Story-telling is a key issue for any understanding of the place of women in the Church and society. The story of the Fall, as mediated in much of Christian tradition, makes women more guilty than men for the fallen condition. Eve becomes the symbol of temptation and the antithesis of Eve, Mary, is too often presented as a woman idealized out of the human condition. However, over the last 200 years women have been able to begin to tell their story through the medium of the novel. This genre has given a voice and access to another version of the story of the human condition. From the controlled irony of Jane Austen and the social comment of Elizabeth Gaskell down through Alice Walker and Mary Gordon, another voice is telling a vital part of the human story. There are myriads of ways of telling a story, so writers shape the material with their personality, their perceptions, their history. Muriel Spark aims at subverting evil by the integrity of her style and tone while Iris Murdoch sees her role as the philosopher telling stories that present the sovereignty of the Good. Other writers open up the world of black women, while Mary Gordon charts the world of American Catholic women as they attempt to wrest their lives from control by priests or parents.

In *The Company of Women* Mary Gordon articulates issues about women's relations to men and especially to clergy. The novel also celebrates the connections, the mutuality, of women's relationships. The novel takes

some lines from W. H. Auden's 'The Common Life' as
its epigraph:

> What draws
> singular lives together in the first place
> loneliness, lust, ambition
> or mere convenience is obvious ...
> How they create through a common world
> between them ...
> no one has yet explained.

The Company of Women goes a long way to explaining,
answering Auden's question. Six women attend a retreat
given by an idiosyncratic priest, Cyprian, and for them he
becomes a focus and much more:

> Still, there was nobody like Cyp, which was why she
> came up here every year. There was something between
> them, between all of them. They were connected to
> something. They stood for something. They were not
> only themselves, secretaries and schoolteachers, people
> who took care of their mothers, ushers in movie
> theatres, the lame ducks no man wanted. When all of
> them came together, they were something.
>
> (*The Company of Women*, p. 28)

Mary Rose, Clare, Muriel, Elizabeth, Charlotte and her
daughter Felicitas become a community drawn initially by
Cyprian and yet growing in mutuality among themselves.
Cyprian calls them his goose girls. He is a man for rules,
railing against laxity in life, in the Church. He is a person of
power and utterly opposed to feelings. When Mary Rose asks
for help in dealing with her violent husband, her perceptions
touch the heart of the man and his power:

> How beautiful his colour was, high red by high
> cheekbones, black hair, brown eyes that she thought
> could see everything. He had forgiven her, but those
> eyes were not forgiving, she could see forgiveness was
> something he had put on with his ordination. He was
> not born to it.
> He was a tall man, a strong man. He could protect
> her or any woman from physical danger. She thought

how good he would have been on the stage.

(p. 43)

Cyprian is on stage most of the time giving monologues, deaf to the real needs of the women who are generous to a fault, caring for his material needs. He taks particular care to inflict his anti-feeling philosophy on Felicitas, still a child. For Cyprian, natural beauty is only a reflection of the divine beauty – it has no meaning in itself. Love of nature for itself is very American, very Protestant. Such is Cyprian's idiosyncratic approach. Felicitas loves the smells of plants and flowers – they are a foretaste of heaven. This infuriates Cyprian, who sees heaven as some Platonic union with the great source of light. So perfumes, fragrances are a distraction and Felicitas has to learn a lesson. He drives her to a farm, and with the help of its decaying owner, she is forced to smell cow dung, chicken droppings and slimy green pig excrement. Felicitas throws up with shock and horror at the abuse, but the event touches her at the core of her being:

> He said to Myron Haber, 'I want to show this lady
> the difference in manures. She says she is interested in
> perfumes.'
>   Then they laughed and Felicitas would always
> remember that laugh. In that laugh she was the other.
> She would know always in that laugh what it was to be
> the outsider, the woman among men, the black among
> whites, the child among adults, the foreigner among
> natives. Always in her life her outrage at injustice
> would bring back those men laughing and the smells
> they made her smell.

(p. 55)

Cyprian wanted her to see that fragrance and natural beauty could keep her from the transcendent light of God.

> and in the motel holding a glass of whisky, 'you must
> hate the world and love God.
>   'And you must not be womanish ... it was womanish
> to believe in happiness on earth, to be a Democrat, to

44

dislike curses, whisky and the smell of sweat ... The
opposite of womanish was orthodox ... Error has
no rights' said Fr Cyprian, explaining why outside the
Church there was no evaluation.

Cyprian's control includes literature. Felicitas is given
books by highly educated Englishwomen – converts. A life
of Cornelia Connolly does little to enthuse her, especially
the story of her youngest child dying after being pushed
into a vat of boiling sugar. 'Felicitas thought it was one
thing to pray for trials but quite another to have your child
caramelised in front of you' (p. 81).

Meanwhile Felicitas is reading Jane Austen secretly because
Cyprian disapproves of reading literature for its own sake.
'The writers of England were not Catholics, they may have
had genius but they were not inspired by the Holy Spirit.
Even Shakespeare for all his greatness could do nothing for
the salvation of even one soul' (p. 93).

> Cyprian was right. It would not lead to the salvation of
> her soul.
> 'What shall I do, since I do love it?' she asked,
> kneeling in the dark.
> 'Read it, if you must, for recreation, but know
> the strict limits of its value. It is not a deeply
> spiritual vision; it cannot be, for it was written in an
> unsanctified age.'
> For the rain it raineth every day.
> She prayed for the voice to be silent. So undependable
> was her mind that she could not keep out songs when
> she was being given vital spiritual counsel, counsel that
> was sacramental in its character, for it took place in the
> great sacrament of penance.
> In her mind, she heard a lute. And then,
> I am slain by a fair cruel maid.
> When she was a young girl, she had changed the words
> to 'I am slain by a fair cruel swain'.
> The more she heard the music, the more certain she
> was that she must work to give it up or to admit that
> its importance was minor.
> She did not even mention Jane Austen in the
> confessional. She did not dare to; Jane Austen's vision

was not, she knew, deeply spiritual. The world of the
spirit was cold and exalted; there was no furniture or
conversation; no jokes no wordplay. The dark night
of the spirit she dreaded as she dreaded walks on
cliffs whose drop was obvious. It was, she knew, her
cowardice that made her wish she was Anne Elliot in
Persuasion, visiting, doing good in ordinary corporal
ways, obedient, grown pale in resignation and lost love.
But where was God in that? And where was God in Mr
Bennet making fun of his poor stupid wife?

(p. 94)

Cyprian manages to make God unattainable for Felicitas
and she sets off to discover love and drugs, finally returning
with a child of her own. Meanwhile the Company of Women
live and grow old around Cyprian, seeming to be controlled
but gradually eroding his control and awakening him to an
awareness that the love of God is sacramental in people. In
all this, Linda the child is the one who becomes the sacrament
of God's love, simple but subversive. The closing lines of the
novel set an agenda of hope not just for the characters in
the novel but perhaps for the Church. Gordon has allowed
the irony of Jane Austen and the warmth of her rectory to
invade the rigidities of Cyprian's cosmos:

Perhaps the greatest grief will be not to see the
child grown. I have never understood women who
grow bored with their children; they must have no
imagination, no interior life. Every question, every
observation I find fascinating; her simple physical
presence is enchanting. Only a week ago, I interrupted
her playing mass. She had memorised some of the
Latin, and she copies my gestures perfectly. For a
moment I was shocked, a girl child saying the sacred
words of God. She asked if I thought she was doing it
well. I said she had learned the Latin perfectly.
  'I'd like to be a priest when I grow up,' she said.
  'You can't,' I said, 'you're female.'
  'So what?' she said, in the tone she defies her
grandmother but not her mother in.
  'Girls can't be priests,' I said. 'Our Lord said so.'

'Where?' she asked.

'In the gospel,' I said.

'Where?' she insisted.

I told her He didn't say it in so many words, but He chose no women to be apostles, and priests are successors to the apostles. That means they would have to be like the apostles.

'But the apostles were Jewish, and you're not Jewish,' she said.

'What's that got to do with it?' I asked her.

'So, you're not like them, and you're a priest.' She glowed with successful argument.

I thought of all the foolish, mediocre men who were permitted ordination because of the accident of their sex. And I thought of this child, obviously superior to all others of her age in beauty, grace and wisdom. I told her to pray that the Church would change its mind by the time she grew up.

'You pray, too,' she said.

I said I would, but it must be a secret between us. And so each morning, at mass, I pray for the ordination of women.

Love is terrible. To disentangle oneself from the passions, the affections, to love with a burning heart which demands only itself and never asks for gratitude or kindness. In that I have failed. I have hungered for kindness; I have hungered for gratitude.

But the love of God, untouched by accident and preference and failure, this I long for. 'Lumen lumens.' The light giving light.

And yet we are incarnate. I look around me at the faces that I love, at the slant, imperfect sun this evening on the mountains, and I pray neither to live nor to die, but to be empty of desire.

(pp. 328–9)

Mary Gordon makes Cyprian a symbol of how the Church and society at large treat women. He is invested with power by his priesthood as part of a hierarchy; he could as easily have been a judge, a policeman, a doctor or any man in a position of authority. He knows he has power when he realizes how he has misused it. He is unable to listen, he just imposes his opinions, able to crush his listeners with his dogma, his judgements, his structures. There is no room in his world for dialogue or exploring feelings. He stands for orthodoxy and dismisses the unreliable nature of feminine choice and experience. He does what he believes is right whatever the cost, he is a loner going against the trend. Yet he can counsel women to be obedient, to be faithful to the letter as well as the spirit of the law. He is happy to form people as he believes they should be, controlling them and deciding what should influence their overall development. He is above all ready to keep people in a state of dependence, unaware of any damage he is doing. His arrogance is indeed massive. Cyprian is, then, a symbol or a living metaphor for the way society, sacred and secular, has been perceived to treat women.

Mary Gordon's novel, by creating this particular closed world, has enabled us to begin to comprehend universal truths. She has appealed to our imagination, to our feelings, our sense of outraged justice and has subverted the system. Men and women have been made to listen to the reality of the misuse of power, not by the marshalling of arguments but by sharing in the rawness of the hurt and the suffering and being appalled by the conspiratorial laughter that pushes anyone with a shred of sensibility to joining those on the margin of life. In the end we realize that Cyprian, because of his intransigence and lack of listening, is like the male-dominated society he stands for: he is the one who is impoverished. He is unwilling to learn. In a reflection of St Mark's Gospel where a Gentile woman asks Jesus to cure her child, Mary Gordon shows Jesus being willing to learn from the faith of the woman and she makes the point: 'We were never allowed to think of Jesus as someone who learned, or grew or developed, particularly in relation to women' (Mary Gordon, 'The Gospel according to St Mark' in *Incarnation*, ed. Alfred Corn (Viking, New York, 1990), p. 17).

A sad commentary: Jesus the founder of Christianity is not imitated in openness by his male disciples!

In the same novel Mary Gordon makes the point that

so-called liberal free-thinking men, as epitomized by the Marxist lecturer Robert Cavendish, are hardly better in their treatment of women. Once the rhetoric of their pronouncements has been penetrated they are as patriarchal as any bishop or judge. Cavendish has his ménage of dependent women and, while they espouse liberal causes and smoke hash, he calls the tune of personal convenience. Felicitas ends up more in love with him than he with her, and when she carries his child his only reaction is to direct her to the abortion clinic. Mercifully, his influence is not paramount and in a harrowing scene at a clinic, Felicitas ends making her choice about her body and the future. Cavendish illustrates the ambivalence of the liberal society that grew out of the 1960s.

In her novels Gordon makes a statement about the dignity of the human person and shows that patriarchy ends up by distorting both men's and women's experiences. What is needed is the acknowledgement of the full and equal humanity of all men and women, and this is rooted in the Gospel. It needs to be made clear then that anything which frustrates equality is an enemy of the Gospel. Those who lord it over others are pagans, not members of the Church. This means that sexism both distorts and hurts, and any work aimed at overcoming such attitudes and practices is part of a work for justice and for the Kingdom.

I have used a novel as a way into this section, as the imagined world enables us to pinpoint the negative dealings between the sexes. However, the negative dealings are themselves based on a travesty of the truth. Over many years woman has been seen both as temptress and as ideal. Woman is either Eve, the prostitute seducing men to sin and wanton weakness, or she is the mother and upholder of impossible ideals. When a woman is raped there is still tremendous confusion of feelings about what has happened. Judges may give lenient sentences to rapists and often imply that in some degree women were responsible. A recent case in Wales where a teenage boy raped a girl resulted in the boy being asked to pay £500 so that his victim could have a holiday. Back at school reports circulated of his peers being impressed by his action. Meanwhile the girl was harassed and criticized. She, the victim, becomes the scapegoat. A recent report shows that many women police officers suffer severe harassment from their male colleagues. Women who complain about gross acts of interference are regarded as whingers and given tougher treatment. It is a sad comment that those who are meant to uphold the law are caught up in such a macho culture. Society loses, because the contribution of women is diminished and possible alternative viewpoints and ways of handling situations are ignored.

The workplace in general is an area where women have guilt imposed on them because of the persistence of fictions. If a married woman succeeds professionally it is assumed that this is done at the expense of her family. People rarely question the harm done by the absence or the indifference of a father. Everything is done to cause conflict between the demands of motherhood and the possibility of continuing a career. The law, medicine and commerce in general display in practice marked indifference to the advancement of women. Beside practical obstacles put in women's paths, other hurdles exist. Some of these problems arise because we have fixed ideas about how women should behave. If a woman is a manager, then her job is to manage and act appropriately. Hard decisions have to be taken, but that does not mean she ceases to be feminine. What we have to reassess is our perception of the feminine – have we made it something weak and unreal? Again the feminine image can be used to exploit women to promote sales of newspapers or consumer goods. Such exploitation maintains the fiction of the feminine and keeps women in the realm of fantasy. A woman can be in the manager's office, but only on a Pirelli calendar.

The daughters of Eve syndrome – the bias of the Genesis story – is certainly alive and well in the Church. Mary Collins, the American theologian, talks about the clerical 'refusal' of women in Roman Catholicism:

Refusal of women is a constitutive mark of the clerical circle, one of the ways clerics define themselves over against other baptised Christians and other human beings. It is essential to the self-definition of clerics that they name maleness as a primary qualification for incorporation into their circle, that they pledge themselves to restrict their associations with women, that they never marry one, and that they understand themselves, in any necessary relations with women, to be superior to them. As a result all associations with women are perceived to be high risk situations because of a fear that there will be a loss of sexual control. In this world-view sins against the chastity of the cleric have the quality of sacrilege. They are seen as profaning of the holy and the desecration of the sacred. (Mary Collins, 'The refusal of women in clerical circles' in *Women in the Church*, ed. Madonna Kolbenschlag
(The Pastoral Press, Washington, DC, 1987))

Mary Collins sees this mentality as part of the organizational baggage the Church acquired from the Greek world. The hierarchically ordered vision gives no status to women except being at the bottom of the pyramid, and this is sexism.

The training of priests reinforces these attitudes and, while in some places attempts have been made to open up the formation of priests to awareness of women, Rome has begun to erect barriers again. As a result, these comments by Mary Collins are still to a considerable degree valid:

The Roman Catholic seminary is one such institution which successfully inculcates this world-view; as such, it is a carefully protected institution. Young men predisposed to the clerical viewpoint for whatever reason are inducted into the Church's clerical ordo step and step [sic] and taught its ways. No curriculum attends to the matter explicitly, but the patterns of seminary life include overt and covert lessons on a necessary suspicion of women as sexual beings and of male superiority to them. Sometimes lessons in contempt have been taught.

(Collins, p. 59)

Reform is needed in this area for the good of all concerned. The ordination of women has become as much a topic in the Catholic Church as in other Christian communities. Rome regards the question as settled, but the debate still goes on. What is interesting in the debate are the perceptions about relationships in the Church that are being raised and also being challenged. Karl Rahner, in volume 20 of his *Theological Investigations*, sees the exclusion of women as essentially rooted in sociological factors. Discrimination against women and a low view of their worth was ingrained, but this vision has nothing to do with revelation. For Rahner the exclusion of women was a human tradition that will change and become obsolete. The Church once accepted slavery without question and now, because of social and cultural change, opposes it. Rahner hopes for development on this question to be analogous to the change in the Church's attitude to religious freedom. He concludes his comments with this respectful plea:

> The Roman Declaration says that in this question the Church must always remain faithful to Jesus Christ. This is of course true in principle. But what fidelity means in connection with this problem remains an open question. Consequently the discussion must continue. Cautiously, with mutual respect, critical of bad arguments on both sides, critical of irrelevant emotionalism expressly or tacitly influencing both sides, but with courage for historical change which is part of the fidelity the Church owes to the Lord.

What Rahner calls for above all on this question is patient dialogue and a challenge about the meaning of fidelity to Jesus. He is asking us all to be willing to be challenged in our perceptions and he will not close the issue. I believe that this issue and its implications have a great deal to do with women's self-worth and the way they are perceived. The general drift of what the Church has to say is so negative that even in attempts to idealize women it is paradoxically undermining them. The present Pope has written on the dignity of women and, while the document is meant to be positive, the feeling that emerges is that a woman is defined as a mother and a wife; any other role is not quite the ideal. This does nothing to help, but can only add to feelings of guilt experienced by women who work from choice or necessity or who are not wives or mothers.

The Benedictine writer Joan Chittister sees the question of ordaining women foundering on a less than adequate notion of the personhood of women. Women, because they are human, are redeemed and therefore called as Ephesians says 'to the riches of his graces'. Why then is one sacrament unavailable to women? Why can they receive Baptism, Confirmation and Eucharist and not the sacrament of Ministry?

Those who have authority in the Church still do not seem to realize that the emergence of women from a position of subordination is one of the twentieth century's most significant themes. Men in general have been slow to acknowledge this reality but, as the world of work and so many other areas of life change, so do the accepted patterns of action. Physical strength and muscle are no longer the prerequisites for work, but what is needed is a more flexible and open-minded approach. The qualities that many women possess, such as team-working, co-operation and imaginative collaboration, are more in evidence. Aggressive styles of management based on power and competition seem to be less acceptable. However, in the world of business and commerce, women still find they encounter glass walls and ceilings, hidden barriers that hinder progress. The difficulty of finding adequate child care can often cause immense stress for women managers and can lead to them giving up work. Lack of child care affects women at every level of work. Women who combine a career and motherhood do make sacrifices and they do not sacrifice their families.

Progress, albeit patchy and with many difficulties including harassment, marks the world of work. In the Church, women have been until recently invisible. But the reality of life in society must impinge on a Church that believes in incarnation. However, while women may officially be invisible, many factors are working for change at grass-roots level. These factors include the changing consciousness of women, their claiming of their own self-worth, needs in the community for ministry that women are answering, and the growing number of women who have received theological formation.

A fascinating debate recently took place in the United States about the Church's attitude to women. Archbishop Weakland OSB of Milwaukee wrote in the *New York Times* on 6 December 1992 that he saw an unwillingness to examine the range of possibilities for women's involvement in the Church. He argued that a closing of the door by the Church on the question of women's ordination could cause massive alienation. Four days later *Catholic New York*, the paper of the diocese of New York, carried a reply by Cardinal O'Connor. The Cardinal made a statement which touched on what is perhaps the core issue when he said 'Archbishop Weakland tends by temperament, it seems to me, to be optimistic about the possibility of cultural harmony between the Church and the world. By temperament, on the contrary, I tend to believe we are in for years and years of confrontation.'

It is true that the wisdom of Christ and the wisdom of the age can be at variance but it is also true that many of society's insights can be endorsed by the Church. Truth is one, and the human mind in its journey is constantly being opened up to new aspects of truth. The Church has been at its best when it has made creative syntheses, not when it has withdrawn and railed against the spirit of the age. The present Pope in his social encyclicals has made it clear that the Church is skilled in dealing with the strivings and needs of humanity. The Vatican Council identified the Christian community with the whole range of human needs and aspirations. Archbishop Weakland called for an ongoing, 'even if painful, dialogue between the Church's tradition and modern insights'. The Archbishop then proposed that the Church should set an example in how it operates its power and jurisdiction by separating them from priestly ordination, so that women could serve the Church at all ranks in its organization in the Vatican. This would mean offices in the Vatican Curia would be open to women. Cardinal O'Connor could see no need for change because the Church is hierarchical, and it is hierarchical because it is apostolic. He rejected any suggestion that he saw women as inferior, but still they remained excluded from priesthood because they were women. Conversely, Archbishop Weakland saw the need for the Church to start a new course, accepting and refining modern insights from the behavioural sciences. If this course were not followed he feared that 'the role of women would be its new Galileo'.

Women have no institutional power in the Church but increasingly they are significantly present in the Church community. Heads of schools, lecturers, professors, retreat givers, ministers to the sick, organizers of parish education programmes: more and more of this missionary work of the Church depends on women. And yet they are still invisible and for much of their activity they depend on the say-so of the Church authorities. Initiatives can be refused or sidelined, and little is done to enable the overall community to accept that these women have a valuable role to play in the life and future of the Church.

The positive side of all this is an interesting paradox and has profound implications. Women have no institutional power in the Church and as a result they do not abuse institutional power. If a woman speaks, her authority has to be based on its clarity and faithfulness to Christ's teaching – she cannot be into coercion or laying down the law. Again, because the ministry of women has never been ritualized, it has the personal quality that is so important if liturgy is to speak to people. The greatest problem can be repersonalizing ritualized ministries. Again, the effect of being on the margin is a greater identification with Jesus. Jesus was not recognized, he was dismissed as being only the carpenter's son, the one who ate with the sinners and the poor.

The position of women in the Church and their dependent ministry makes Christianity more of the counter-culture that it is meant to be. Like Jesus they can proclaim the way of gentleness and love and realize that in Jesus there is absolute fulfilment. Whenever we meet and tell the story, then we have Church and the source of grace. The power of the sacraments comes from God's love, and we do not have to get obsessed about the 'how' of sacraments. It is the memory of Christ that brings grace and makes the Church the community of salvation. The Eucharist is the place where the people are gathered and the story of Jesus is told and we are open to his healing of reality.

The way to healing from the negative, in society and the Church, lies in finding Jesus as the key to absolute fulfilment. It is he who takes us up into the richest community, the inner life of God, and by the Spirit we find the source of wisdom and love. Many of the sufferings we experience assault our hope but if we are willing to be open to the salvation of Jesus then we acquire a largeness of heart. The reality of the life of Jesus and the encounters we have with him free us from human limitations and take us up into the divine transcendence. This means that in the midst of the darkness of problems with the institution and all sorts of control, God becomes God for us and, in the words of John of the Cross, we can go out and find the beloved. John found God in his prison. It was there he found his lyric voice and he was able to escape from unjust structures.

It is vital to root ourselves in a deep and meaningful spirituality because it enables us to know we gain our self-worth from God and no one can take this from us. It also means that we view the Church primarily as the sacrament of Christ. Although it is an institution its basic reality is the mediating of Christ and realizing the Kingdom of God – the ways of God breaking out in the world.

We need a spirituality that can dream of alternatives. A big problem is that much masculine spirituality has projected some variants of male development onto God which can be alienating for both men and women. A vision of God as remote, above it all and impassive, makes us ask: 'How can this remote person be concerned with me?' Yet we know that in reality Jesus shared our suffering on the cross. God is present in tragedy, in suffering. If we only see God as powerful we can too easily justify our use of power to cause suffering.

There is danger in the concept that God is distant and outside the mess of ordinary life. It may make us see God as some kind of exalted Emperor with powers to punish that produce reactions of fear and anxiety. It is this sort of picture of God projected from male images that can cause deep anxieties and become a source of alienation to both men and women. Kingsley Amis in his novel *The Anti-Death League* sees God as the author of random mischance enjoying the range of possible discomforts at his disposal. Amis associates sudden death and all the nastiness in life as coming from a powerful indifferent being. He writes with a Swift-like savagery but his underlying theme reflects the feeling many people can have about an image, a perception of God outside and above the world.

The other danger of images of God standing over the world, exercising power over it, is that they can be transferred to the shaping of institutions in our society. The notion of 'lording it over' is one that meets with the sharpest rebukes from Jesus, who sees the misuse of power as pagan, a sign of an unredeemed society. For Jesus, authority is seen in service, and he reminds us that 'the one who is first among you should be as your servant'. We see Jesus acting on this in the washing of the disciples' feet at the Last Supper. Gospel incidents also remind us that the early Christian community took great care to be a community of brothers and sisters. They did not envisage a rigid hierarchy; order does not require rigidity.

The early Christian community was a community of the Spirit. The Spirit was the enabling of God from within the person or within the group. The spirit gives us access to the Father, and the Spirit is the bond that makes us into the Communion that is the Church. Jesus lived his mission in and through the Spirit and it is in the same power of love that we find intimacy with God and one another.

One of the results of women's exclusion from power in the Church is that they and all of us look critically at power structures and seek alternatives. Looking for alternatives needs imagination, the realization that reality need never be expressed by any one view. The more both men and women can identify with Jesus as the servant, the one who was on the margin, the more the Church will conform to the Gospel. Furthermore, it was in the Spirit that his ministry was fulfilled as 'the servant in whom I am well pleased'.

Those who are on the margin and excluded from the public domain in the Church have more to offer. Public skills can easily be learnt, whether they be of management or other organizational functions, but private skills are in the end crucial and need long experience to acquire. The capacity to listen and really understand people grows out of long experience and is also rooted in prayer. The contemplative, the person who waits on God, is far more likely to be understanding of people's needs because they have learnt to let God be God in their lives. This means they will be more alive to the good in others and be able to hear the crucial story which we must hear if we are going to help others. Again, in working with groups, awareness of the tone of a complex situation is a highly sensitive ability that is not learnt overnight. If we are to develop such skills we have to enter situations listening and open, poor in spirit. We cannot go in with our agenda, our blueprint, our decision about where truth and error reside.

The sad fact is that decision-making in the Church does exclude women. Women religious have no role in policy-making about their lifestyle. Rome is often very anxious to legislate, for example, about how women religious dress. This anxiety to control says something about perceptions of women's sexuality. Decisions about dress should be decisions taken by women, otherwise there is a hint of the totalitarian. Margaret Attwood in her novel *The Handmaid's Tale* presents a society where women have lost all their rights including freedom to choose how they dress. All this is done to protect this particular society from too much freedom.

If women religious have no role in policy-making, neither do women generally have any input into papal encyclicals on social or moral questions. Areas that touch on the world of work, family life and sexuality are basic human experiences, but no procedure exists for hearing the evidence of half the human race. The American bishops have over the last few years attempted to listen to women. They wanted to write a joint pastoral where they could speak to women and address the issues that they had heard. The consultation was a long and sensitive process but in the end they did not publish the pastoral. The draft document was criticized and subjected to emendations. The bishops then felt that the emended document, which now seemed to go against their consultation, would not be worth publishing. It would not achieve positive results.

Women are often the exploited workforce, they have to sustain family life and hand on Christianity. I believe that the exclusion of women from leadership roles in the Church is another way they are de-skilled and have self-worth eroded. If the Church is to be a servant Church speaking to a needy world, it needs to be more humane and less apparently authoritarian. It is precisely here that women's ways of acting are needed, mutuality, interdependence, the sense of connectedness. Perhaps the greatest barrier to change in the Church is the fact that the architects of our civilization have all been men: Aristotle, Aquinas, Kant, Darwin, Freud, Marx and Einstein. It is all too easy for the Church to accept the conventions of society but as the Church must be a counter-culture, it must go beyond the wisdom of the age. This gives hope because, if the Church is true to its deepest mission, it will hear the groanings of its members and allow alternative ways of being to emerge.

5

□

The quick fix

□

The burden of trying to sort out all the rights and wrongs of our lives – in business, in our personal relationships and in the church – can be too much for us. It can all seem too complicated. More and more people seem driven to searching for a quick, simple solution. Give me an answer and then I can get on with the business of living, or perhaps I mean leave me alone. This approach is common both in Church circles and in society in general. The simplified solution is sought, conscience is anaesthetized and life can continue on a smooth course especially in the public domain. It would seem we can bear neither too much reality nor too much responsibility. But correct behaviour and simple solutions can lead to a frightening society.

Margaret Attwood presents a society where everything has been simplified. The world of *The Handmaid's Tale*, set some fifty years in the future, is a totalitarian regime built on the ruins of our contemporary liberalism. It is a society reacting to too much choice, which protects its citizens against 'freedom from' but does not allow 'freedom to'. *The Handmaid's Tale*, like P. D. James's *The Children of Men*, describes a world where human fertility has become a problem: in Attwood's world birth is rare, for James an omega point has marked the end of human reproduction. Both novels imagine worlds that follow from the sexual freedom of our day, and the consequences implied are dire. The worlds that we see in these novels are not Prospero's 'brave new world' but societies cramped by control and shaped by secret police. In *The Handmaid's Tale*, the coup that turns America into a theocracy like contemporary Iran is relatively simple to effect and the message is that there are enough people around who would accept a simplified society, provided that they were the decision-makers and not those who were being dragooned into correctness.

The lure of the simple solution does, I think, arise from a sense of a void in our society. Politicians are calling on the Church to teach morality, when they are shocked by sane people's behaviour. At the same time many people feel empty, and deeply depressed. The complexities of life bring especially those who try to serve the community – doctors, social workers, teachers, nurses, police and clergy – to the brink. Suicide, depression, opting out, are the ways many of them react. The stress, tension and pressure are beyond people's resources. In a society that is dominated by the market concept in which life is quantified, people's effectiveness is judged as part of a financial and not a human equation. The result is that those who are in the caring professions are stressed and stretched beyond their capacity. Many of the police who dealt with the aftermath of the Zeebrugge shipwreck have resigned from the force, and fewer and fewer police stay on to retirement. Teachers faced with classroom violence, financial administration and more and more complex assessment procedures feel drained of energy and enthusiasm. The same can be said of doctors and other professionals, who deal primarily with people but who are now subject to a complicated system designed to stimulate the market. We are all purchasers and providers, but where are the values and who knows the cost? People have been loaded with amazing burdens which make it difficult to live as human beings. The liberal capitalist model with the profit motive as its guiding principle has come to dominate our Western world, outweighing all other values.

For many people today, there is a form of religion which gives simple answers to our questions; it has the respectability of orthodoxy and it takes away feelings of guilt and anxiety. 'I will give my life over unconditionally to ...' – and the sentence can be completed by a whole host of possibilities.

Fundamentalism is a reaction to a perceived growth of liberalism in the religious sphere. It is primarily an evangelical phenomenon, but over the last few years it has spilled over into other traditions. Fundamentalism is a complex of realities, it is a mind-set, a cultural and socio-political framework as well.

As a way of confronting reality, fundamentalism appeals to people who by temperament would incline to be dogmatic, cut and dried. They want a clear answer and they want to be in a club where the rules are defined. This kind of person would be keen on a rigorist approach to moral questions. In the Catholic tradition people of this mind-set would want to name actions as being mortal sins. Divorce, contraception, not kneeling for communion are all grist to the rigorist mill. Catholic fundamentalists would be clear that there is no salvation outside the Church. What the word 'Church' means would vary but in the end it would be a very exclusive body. Whenever I think of an exclusive body I picture a particular spot in Canterbury. Walking along the city walls just west of the Burgate you find the Church of the Strict and Particular Baptists. Nestling as it does in the shadow of the Cathedral, this tiny chapel that could hold not more than a dozen symbolizes a vision of an exclusive elect. Such an exclusive vision runs counter to Christ's vision of the Kingdom where all are called from east to west, sinners and virtuous alike. The rigorist, exclusive mentality is best caught in Samuel Butler's evocative novel *The Way of All Flesh*. Here the unfortunate Ernest Pontifex is subjected to a fundamentalist upbringing which scars and in the end almost breaks him. This echoes much of Butler's own upbringing, and the novel is a good illustration of attitudes that live on among certain Christian groups.

Another aspect of the fundamentalist mentality is a literal approach to reality. What is in print or what a particular group endorses is sacrosanct. The text of Scripture or the message of some revelation become everything. Among Catholics, the secret of Fatima can attain an importance that goes beyond the Gospels. This secret goes along with an apocalyptic scenario that will only be averted if certain prayers and practices are carried out. In pastoral care I find that such focusing on private revelations can remove people from the realities of daily life into what can be almost a fantasy life. Furthermore, once anyone is caught up in enthusiasm for some special revelation, the danger is that they stay inside the limited circle of those who believe in the message. People reinforce each other's beliefs and anyone who is unwilling to buy in is regarded with feelings ranging from pity to hostility. What I have always noticed is that those who become crusading in these matters rarely seem fulfilled, but rather add to their level of anxiety.

An interesting fundamentalist coalition that includes a wide spectrum of denominations is the more aggressive part of the anti-abortion lobby. Groups like Rescue America have a rigorist stance against anything or anybody associated with abortion. Their opposition to abortion leads them to feel free to take any measures in their power to prevent abortions taking place. This opposition includes physical violence, destruction of buildings and harassment. I am myself against abortion but I do not believe that I can use any means to force my views on people. I believe in dialogue and persuasion but I have, even if I disagree, to respect a person's decision. The authority of Christ lay in the clarity of his teaching, not in any imposition of his views. It is interesting to note that some anti-abortion groups show a lack of consistency in their crusade for life. Radical anti-abortion groups (and I do not include Life or SPUC), as with many fundamentalist groups, operate out of a right-wing political agenda. This agenda would include support for the death penalty and a willingness to use weapons of mass destruction if it suited their opposition to a perceived enemy. I would hold that respect for life has to be all-inclusive. It is interesting to note that for the early Christians, 'thou shalt not kill' meant not getting involved in the military machine of the Roman Empire.

Fundamentalism in the last twenty years or so has acquired a right-wing political overtone. Both in the United States and Britain, a literal view of the Bible and its teaching has been buttressed by right-wing views. The fundamentalist approach is of individual salvation, and the politics of the right stress the individual over against society or the community. Being poor is the fault of the poor individual and there is no problem in justifying the acquisition of wealth. The good Samaritan was generous because he had the money to be generous. The message of personal salvation is reassuring but it is rarely accompanied by any reference to the needs of the community or the need to challenge the sinful structures of society. John McDade writes in *The Month* (March 1993):

> There is no such thing as *private morality* as though it can be distinguished from *public morality*. All morality is both private and public, it has an individual focus as well as a public expression, just as all sin is both public and social. The removal of sin cannot be achieved without at the same time removing the conditions which come from sin and which continue to promote destructive behaviour.

The political right and the fundamentalists both appeal to tradition as they fend off what they regard as untenable in modern life. The tradition they appeal to is often from the recent past rather than the very sources of Christianity – in Britain Victorian values have been called upon. The appeal to tradition and the values so enshrined are an attempt to use religion to legitimize the *status quo*. It is also a way of manipulating religion so that it becomes a palliative rather than a prophetic and liberating force. When the Church offers a liberating message or advocates change, this is opposed as interference. However, if a Church, in its opposition to the modern, proclaims certain simple doctrines linked to an endorsement of a political agenda, then it will appeal to those who feel uncomfortable in modern society.

It is this element of fundamentalism that is appealing: the offer of security to those who feel unhappy, uncomfortable, out of place in contemporary society and who want an alternative. For some people an alternative is change and challenging what is negative in the *status quo*. For others the feeling is that in contemporary society they are beleaguered and ridiculed and so they would like to associate with like-minded folk. It is groups like this that feel most at home in a fundamentalist church setting. Here doctrines are clearly agreed and the Church is a refuge from all that is perceived as nasty. Above all, members of such churches are given assurance of salvation which means that, provided they have handed over their lives to God, all is sure.

Another factor that contributes to the fundamentalist scene is the way such churches gradually drift away from their denominational base and become outsiders to the common religious culture of the day. This means that separatist churches cut off from mainstream leadership depend more and more on the leaders thrown up at the local level. The problem here is that so often a forceful personality takes over. Such leaders can be extremely authoritarian and, as a church, members can be subject to rigid and doctrinaire teaching with very little possibility of disagreement. In this sort of context human development is cramped and members of church communities are often manipulated.

However, while fundamentalism is not a solution, it is important not to underestimate its influence nor the effort that fuels such groups. While they disapprove of the modern world they are very much at home with modern technology, which they use to spread their message. They are also good at picking up where people's concerns are – they have good antennae. Using organizational skills and good planning they are extremely effective in getting their message to a wide public. Again it would be wrong to see fundamentalists as traditionalists. In a world of doubt and uncertainty they are very good at building up an alternative world which they validate by rooting it in a sacred tent. Community is built up and bonds are forged by using political ideology; what is happening is a process of selection and identity construction. This construction has the appeal of being trustworthy in a world that is hostile, immoral and uncertain. The trust they provide inoculates, and screens out potential threats. A quality of faith and life is guaranteed and its purity is underwritten by the Lord's abiding presence.

Besides the attraction of fundamentalist church groups there are also cults that attract more and more adherents. The word 'cult' indicates a group that has a religious bias but is regarded by mainstream religion with some suspicion. 'Cults are always them and never us' (Shirley Harrison, *Cults* (London, 1990), p. 9). Cults demand not just commitment but, it would seem, almost addiction to the movement. Once you become a member then barriers appear between you and your former life, you and your family.

The movements that would be classified as cults would be organizations like the Unification Church (Moonies) and the Scientologists. Cults recruit on the street, on the university campus. They target people who are lonely or in a state of crisis and offer them friendship, a caring community and instant access to God. Often such groups have powerful leaders who exploit members both financially and psychologically. Once caught up into the movement, it is hard to leave. Some cults end in disaster, while others, such as the Unification Church, have developed a structure that has enabled them to survive even hostile government investigations.

Cults and fundamentalist groupings will have an increasing fascination as we approach the end of the century. The millennium is a time that evokes powerful feelings in the human psyche and doubtless groups will flourish proclaiming the end of the world. The sense of an ending is part and parcel of human life: endings are little deaths that cause grief. Endings are also gates to new beginnings: for Christians death is the gateway to resurrection. However, if the resurrection factor is missing then endings, millenniums, can be causes of anxiety. It will be in this sort of context that the next few years will doubtless see a growth in cults and other religious groups. The geopolitical scene will also enhance such problems. The new world order is fraught with uncertainty. The response includes a return to nationalism in the narrowest sense, and such nationalism often includes a religious element that has more to do with a past culture than a living faith.

The lure of fundamentalism, the need for quick-fix religion to solve problems, is a growth industry but, I believe, a blind alley. Has mainstream Christianity in its teaching, its worship, its pastoral care, a way that will speak to humanity and help us become more human, more alive? I believe it has, and I would like to round off my thoughts with what I would hope is a modest but positive contribution.

6

□

A vision of wholeness

□

'The truth will set you free.'

'Behold, I make all things new.'

The Gospel message is one of freedom, but how do we
ground it in the reality of life now, so that it is a source of
hope? We need reminders, models, to tell us that holiness
and wholeness are possible for human beings. I believe that
we have a dignity that is God-given and that we can live and
act as responsible persons. I would agree with Kevin Kelly
that a crucial barrier to our growth and personal development
is a misinterpretation of original sin. Kelly refers to the 'lie of
original sin' which is basically a refusal to accept that God
believes in us and that human nature is open to change
and growth in goodness. Life and human nature are not
set in negative and predetermined patterns. Creation and
redemption are in the end part of the overall process of
reality coming into being.

The insights of the behavioural sciences, which are a significant development in this century, help in the building of a
positive vision of the human person. Areas of our personality
which have often been misunderstood can be seen positively
and our basic unity can be affirmed. We can only function as
human beings when we acknowledge the unity of body, mind
and soul and reject once and for all the negative antithesis of
body and soul, spirit and matter. I am not a soul trapped in
a body: it is as a bodily, and that means as a sexual, person
that I achieve union with God.

What we need is to rediscover our basic worth as God-given

and to realize that our calling is to holiness. Holiness is a wholeness that is achieved as we build creative relationships with God and our fellow human beings. God wants our happiness, our fulfilment, both in this world and in the next. How do we achieve that, how do we move away from oppressive anxiety and adversarial guilt? Any answer to such a question cannot be facile or naïvely optimistic. We have to admit bias, tension and the limitations of being finite. But we can change, we can help each other, and as Christians we believe that grace builds on nature. Our life, as Peter Selby has stated, is a combination of majesty and disaster. We need to be in touch with the emptiness and the glory. Peter Selby compares us to children learning to walk. Sometimes we rush along with the excitement life engenders, at other times we trip and fall for no apparent reason. Like children we need to get up and see the mistake, the over-reaching, as a time to learn, not as a failure to be heaped all over us. We need help to grow, to stand and fall; we need the right environment and we need to be understood with compassion.

Compassionate listening is the key to real growth. Compassion is more than empathy or being alongside someone in their need, it is an involvement deep enough to make us feel our innards churning. The Bible speaks of the bowels of compassion, to show how deep that feeling is. Suffering with, feeling the pain, would be another way to begin to describe what it entails. Listening means a willingness to be open to life and to learn from experience. It takes us away from the analytical logical explanation of events. It respects the uniqueness of the person. When we fail to listen we name events according to our preconceptions and prejudices, refusing to know and understand the needs, the problems and where the other person really is. Knowing the meaning of the question prevents us supplying inadequate and imperfect answers. Compassionate listening springs from respectful relationships, it is far removed from power, condemnation and censure. So often we apply logic to life, trying to fit the complexity of human behaviour into what can only be a partial analysis. Life is larger than logic and compassion leads to a vision based on a justice that exceeds the narrow bands of legalism.

We need to be helped into compassion and such help is

68

found in the life of the Church in the sacrament that we call Confession. This is one of the seven sacraments celebrated in the Catholic Church and it is the time when an individual goes before a priest, who stands in the place of Christ to mediate Christ's compassion and to enable those in need to feel that they can be welcomed back into a renewed friendship with God and their neighbour and rediscover their self-worth. The sacrament as a positive healing aspect of our lives and growth can be more important than many people realize. For someone with a positive commitment to God and a desire to attain wholeness this sacrament is crucial. It is not to be confused with counselling, but it can form part of an overall strategy for achieving that human growth and healing which is at the heart of the Gospel.

Jesus is the sacrament of God's reconciling love, he is the embodiment of compassion. It is this reconciling, healing, compassionate love that is the reality of the sacrament of reconciliation. Jesus is the one who could not bear to see people lost, wandering, alienated. He wanted everyone to find a right relation with the Father. Jesus, as the compassion of God, releases the energy that will restore right relations between humanity and God. If we are right with God then we will find peace with each other.

At the core of the process of reconciliation there are two mysteries: on the one hand there is God's forgiveness, on the other is sin. Why should we be so unreasonable in our foolishness and why should God be so concerned about us?

God's forgiveness, his desire to love and heal us, is something we find difficult to accept. Images of God as judge and our anxieties crowd out the possibility of the power of forgiveness. We feel shame or believe that our situation is beyond redemption. In part this feeling can come from depression. It also has roots in an idea that God is angry because of our sinfulness and that we are on the road to perdition. What we need to do is to believe that Jesus in his life and teaching embodies what God has to say about forgiveness. The reality of sin as unreasonable foolishness is and must be taken as objective, but the condition of the sinner is something else. Jesus cannot bear to leave people at odds with the Father and, as the Father's Spirit works in and through him, his actions show the divine forgiveness.

His Father is not someone who needs appeasing but, rather, he is the one who begins the work of our salvation.

When we find ourselves caught up in negative behaviour, in culs-de-sac of our own making, in states of conflict and unresolved tensions, God working through Jesus shows profound sympathy with our suffering. Jesus is deeply concerned about the damage sin does to us as individuals but he also understands where we are. We often cling to sin because we believe that this is the only way life can be. Jesus in turn not only preaches the need to repent but offers us the treasure, the pearl of great price. The rule of God within our hearts and minds is his message. Jesus stresses the beauty of the alternative to sin, showing that this is what our Father wants for us. We only have to risk allowing God freedom in our lives.

We need to accept our woundedness and to allow the creative work of forgiveness into our being. The dynamic of forgiveness is about the change that can happen in us as persons. We are not bad, but we can so often allow ourselves to be content with being less than human. We choose that which suits only ourselves, denying relationships and satisfying our feelings and instincts in a totally thoughtless way. Sin leads us to an isolated existence that lacks a sense of trust and is dominated by self-interest at all costs. In the evolutionary view of human nature, sin is allowing the reflex animal aspect of our nature to have an appropriate dominance. The instinct for survival and the stirrings of our appetites can only find authentic expression in relationships with others. My well-being is not to be achieved at any cost, nor my appetites gratified without reflecting on the appropriateness of the need. I cannot push, shove, elbow and trample through life. If others live that way, trying to compete with them is a recipe for greater conflict and chaos.

The basis for positive behaviour and growth is an awareness of who I really am. What is the source of my real worth? What is the ground of my dignity? The opening of the letter to the Ephesians speaks powerfully to these questions: 'Thus he chose us in Christ before the world was made, to be holy and faultless before him in love ... chosen to be, for the praise of his glory' (see Ephesians 1:4–12). Later in the same letter Paul declares, 'We are God's work of art, created in Christ Jesus for the good works which God has already designated to make up our way of life' (Ephesians 2:10).

From the beginning God has created us to be in a relationship of love and positive living. The creating and redeeming work of God in Christ is at the source of our life and all we do. The question is how far can we believe this, how positive are we in accepting and living out this message? Hearing the good news needs a willingness to go beyond how we have been accustomed to think and pray. These insights that Paul gives us can only be accepted if we allow ourselves to be opened up to the dramatically different view of reality that lies at the heart of the New Testament. We need to let go of previously held convictions and be willing to practise a radical detachment whereby our vision of ourselves and how we live is challenged and changed. It is this type of detachment that St John of the Cross tries to communicate in his poems. We pass through a purification where we encounter God on God's terms and discover that our value lies in the reality of God loving us unconditionally. The follow-up of that truth is the realization that God also desires the same relationship with every human being. If we see human worth and value in such a light then crudeness in relationships, bitter competition, will no longer have any meaning.

However, it takes time to gain this mentality, which is a part of the process of conversion. We need to listen to the Scriptures and allow God's word to percolate through our being, and to work at understanding ourselves and our actions. Too often we name actions as sins but fail to remember that they reflect aspects of our personality as it is and the overall quality of our response to God. Do we live with the grain of God's love or does self-directed activity make us go against the grain? Where do we need to let go, to lose our control and allow the new creation to flourish? It's too easy to brood over the past. We need the courage to forgive ourselves and move on.

What changes do we need to make to enable reconciliation to take place in our society? This leads us on to reflect on structural sin. The very way that we organize our society is so often according to a wisdom that lacks love and is based on the short-term, the purely pragmatic, the useful — Mary Grey

71

has called sin the uncreating process and sees structural sin as the way society endorses the uncreating process. It means that society is organized in such a way as to deny principles that work for the common good. The bias is in favour of the powerful and the poor are reduced to victims. When we live in a society that is going in a direction contrary to the Gospel, it is hard for the individual to live the truth. I hear one message in church, yet life around me is an apparent contradiction.

Respect for the person is the key to a just society and that certainly is the way forward in all areas of morality. A good sexual ethic flows from my own sense of worth and my unwillingness to use or abuse others. One of the most common ways we violate persons is by a constantly critical attitude. We de-skill people by a negative superiority and, also, the criticism has a corrosive effect on all concerned. Such behaviour is all too common especially among closed groups, and the sharp-tongued perpetrator can often exercise a reign of terror in a group. When I use people to gratify my needs and dominate them, I harm their self-image and damage their dignity. This using of people can range from casual sex to seeing someone as useful in advancing my career or social standing. Men often like to have the adornment of a pretty woman as a sign of their all-round prowess, while others name-drop. There is a whole scale of using people; it is often done almost unconsciously, but very often it is fuelled by a misplaced power drive. In all of this there is an amazing amount of self-deception because the more we allow power to motivate our dealings, the less able we are to see clearly.

But living this life of self-deception can be an immense mental strain. How can we live with ourselves and others if we are never genuine in what we do? A life that is unexamined and driven by greed can drift into the most appalling selfishness and brutality. Atrocities are usually committed by sane people who have allowed their sensitivity to be atrophied. The heedless pursuit of self-interest leaves people blind and deaf to the plight of others. The wisdom of the age can lead us to accept the unacceptable as the norm.

It is in this context that we need some impetus to move us away from a closed selfish world into a context of healing, where the experience of compassion will enable us to become compassionate ourselves. The awareness of the foolishness and futility of our behaviour is healthy guilt. Healthy guilt is the awareness breaking in on our life that this mode of living is getting us nowhere − it is the sense that our behaviour is intolerable. It is as if we see our face in a mirror unexpectedly and we do not like the reflection. We feel at odds, uneasy, no longer comfortable with our way of living. This is guilt that can be the prelude to radical change and healing. Guilt in this context is a healthy dissatisfaction, it becomes an agent of change. It is totally different to a sense of being driven or anxious; in fact, paradoxically, it can free us from such negative responses.

The recognition that we need healing as we react to the awareness that our life is misdirected is the prelude to reconciliation. I see the celebration of the sacrament of reconciliation as our opportunity to meet the compassion of God mediated into our lives through Jesus. The sacrament of reconciliation redirects us on our faith journey and enables us not just to name sins, but to be helped to discover both who we are and how God wants to be in our lives. From the moment we have been involved in the foolishness of sin God has wanted to heal us. By his very life Jesus is the clear statement of that desire; now it is up to us to grasp the help.

For many people the sacrament of reconciliation, or Confession as it is still so often called, is an off-putting experience. The sacrament seems a fearsome, nerve-racking event. It is also felt to be quite a confusing experience. What do I do? What do I say? Do I need to have a list of sins? Will the priest be understanding? And behind it all is a deep worry about how God is feeling about me. Going to confession and going to the dentist are about on a par in terms of positive response. The other perception that is present is the sense that I am before some judgement seat: will I be found wanting?

But the sacrament of reconciliation is not just the act of confessing sins. This has assumed a disproportionate role. Reconciliation is a time of healing, growth in freedom and a renewal of our basic option for God. We see as we reflect on our lives how God's grace has enabled us, but we also see where our temperamental bias and our limitations have brought us. We can use this opportunity to turn our foolishness into forgiveness and freedom. When we meet Christ in this sacrament we gain strength to keep on with our journey, and the whole encounter enables us to give meaning to what we are doing. It frees us from burdens and gives positive directions. We see how often we can behave in an unreflective and instinctual way that ignores the needs of others and, while seemingly we are gratified, in fact we become more isolated and alienated. This makes us realize that a vital element of the sacrament is the way it makes us aware that our behaviour is never private – someone else is also diminished by what we do. If I sin, the witness of the Church is diminished, it is less a light to the nations. Celebrating the sacrament is a time when we raise our consciousness, and the priest, listening prayerfully, enables us to make connections and open up to God. The priest for his part is conscious of his woundedness and he operates not from any position of superiority but rather as a brother serving others so that they may have life in abundance. Sadly, many people have not always had a good experience of a priest being understanding in confession. This lack of sympathy is often brought out in portrayals of priests in novels where they can be indifferent, insensitive or inquisitive. Graham Greene, in his portrayal of the priest as confessor, does have priests who are indifferent, but most of his priests in the confessional are harbingers of hope and express the friendship of Christ.

Many people who come to the sacrament come with immense anxieties and also for some the event is a risk. They feel on the margin. People feel outsiders and nervous because they often hear sweeping condemnations that make them feel as if they have no hope. When a marriage ends in divorce it is often the partner who has tried to live by the Gospel who feels most blameworthy. Where did I go wrong or fail to give that extra something to the relationship? Can I still be a member of the Church after all this has happened? Added to those feelings there is also the problem that the sun *does* go down on my anger because there are feelings of bitterness about the deceit and hurt that accompany marital breakdown. A married person may be cast aside with never a word, and feel that they are pushed to one side as if they have passed their sell-by date. How do we find reconciliation in that context? I believe that the sacrament will be the beginning of a process of healing. The priest, in the name of the community, will need to reassure such a person that the Church, as the presence of Christ, cares and above all directs the person towards the counselling and support they need. People need time, and those hurting after rejection want to meet the compassion of Christ. I always try and make it clear that finding a network of care for someone in need is a priority, and I do all I can to dispel any fear that demands should not be made on my time. The sacrament, for a person who is wounded because of injustice and callousness, has to be a door of welcome back into life and wholeness.

Gay Catholics must feel the Church gives ambivalent signals and the tone of Roman documents must sound heavy and condemnatory. However, statements by the Church in the English-speaking world are becoming much more pastorally caring and it is to be hoped that they will enable gay Catholics to take their place in the community – not to feel alienated.

The sacrament of reconciliation must be an opportunity for creative encounter and healing help. We are designed for relationships – we are all meant to know our worth as God's work of art and so we must see our sexuality as a dynamic in the realization of our wholeness and not as a negative factor. To suggest that being gay is in some way to be less a person is to usurp God's role and also to claim to know more about the mystery of the person than the Creator. I believe very strongly in affirming people's basic goodness as they come to the sacrament, and then helping them to be open to the healing and creative power of God's grace. What matters is the integrity and respectfulness of our relationships.

Many other people come to confession feeling at odds and alienated because they have struggled and then it seems they have failed. The ideal of being a good Catholic and a good Christian seems unattainable – something only possible for the respectable. Holiness is trying to make sense of the mess, but we have often made it seem as if it was about getting it all right. So often such folk will talk about being angry with God, and I would say that if they let that anger out to God it would be the beginning of authentic prayer. Telling God you're fed up and the whole Church thing is an intolerable burden can be the healthiest possible reaction. I believe we all have to remember that our prayers go to a God who in Jesus has been through it all from exhaustion to depression. It is vital that we remember that Jesus, though he was divine, was fully human and, therefore, he experienced the whole range of human emotions and the challenges of life. In his glorified state Jesus is still in touch with all these human experiences and when we pray out of our difficulties he feels with us from his own experience. I find that such a way of relating to Jesus gives much greater meaning to my prayer. Such a God knows the unreasonable demands of institutions and systems and wants us to move into a personal liberating friendship. Keeping a marriage afloat, bringing up children, coping with financial demands, holding down a job, it is here that holiness is found and that is where we need strength and healing. Our tiredness, shortcomings and short cuts in the pressure of life are not failures, they are the limitations of being finite. The sacrament of reconciliation wants us to say that it is in the fragile edges of our life that God's healing life will enable us.

The healing work of the sacrament of reconciliation is not just an individual affair. As a community we need healing, and an essential part of the Christian community's life is to admit its constant need of reformation.

The revised rite of the sacrament of reconciliation, while envisaging a deeper relationship with Christ through the individual celebration of the sacrament, also makes provision for communal celebration. Here we gather as a community where we affirm that even though our sin may be secret it is never private. It affects the whole community. Our presence together at such a celebration is an admission of the woundedness we share and we become conscious of the fact that our individual foolishness clouds the witness of the community. Such celebrations enable us to admit as a group our need for help and then as individuals we ask for the particular strength we need for the next stage of the journey. On such occasions I find that the individual reconciliation can be accompanied by a symbolic gesture that springs from the listening to Scripture that forms part of such a service.

The symbolic gesture can take many forms. The use of water can be potent: as we go to the priest we can bathe our eyes in water and then, as we say what has blinded us to God's love, the priest wipes our eyes and absolves. Again, writing down the reality that blocks love and then burning the paper shows the decisive change of forgiveness. Another symbol can be dropping a pebble into a bowl of water to show the negative baggage we want to cast aside, so we are no longer held down by the weight of guilt or anxiety. Such celebrations, linked to the great feasts, can have enormous power and help us see others as sharing the pain and joy of being human, putting on Christ.

The process of healing or being reconciled is also a coming of age, a taking of responsibility for our lives. Negative guilt and anxiety can often hold us in a prison which in a paradoxical way can be strangely congenial. As long as I am locked in this state I have the perfect alibi for not engaging with life. We need great trust in God working in us as we allow ourselves to live and discover the freedom that is the other side of all the brokenness that has hitherto cramped and even paralysed our lives.

I said earlier on that the sacrament of reconciliation was not to be confused with counselling or spiritual direction. However, the sacrament can often be for Christians a window of opportunity. I often find that the person I meet in the sacrament needs not only the assurance of God's help but also the binding up of psychological hurt, and hence as a confessor I could well suggest the help of a counsellor or spiritual director, depending on the need. Sometimes a support group like the Association for Separated and Divorced Catholics can be invaluable. What is happening is that the Gospel as lived in the sacrament is pointing to connections that need to be made in that person's life.

People need more than the dry performance of a rite. In many cases they do need counselling or spiritual direction too. But there is a need to find the right kind of help. If people mistrust the Church or feel it has no answer for their personal problems, they will hunt for gurus and place their faith in alternatives. The last twenty or thirty years have seen the rise and fall of a whole host of gurus and alternatives. Schools of meditation, group therapy, counselling, are all tried as possible avenues and yet found wanting. Some of the more exotic groups have proved to be exploitative and frauds. The whole scene of counselling and therapy has become a convenient ground of operation for some practitioners who are scarcely qualified to effect their promises. The intimate relation set up in therapy is too easily open to abuse and exploitation. Again, some clients can pile inordinate expectations on a counsellor and often forget that counselling is one element in the process of achieving integrity and integration.

Kingsley Amis in his novels *Jake's Thing* and *Stanley and the Women* has, by his satire, exposed the shortcomings of the world of therapy. He would see therapy, whether group or individual, as an intrusion that is unwarranted and usually ineffective. On the other hand, what his novels also show is an enormous amount of self-destructive behaviour and denial in his characters who reject therapy. Jake Richardson, the self-indulgent don who rages against therapy, has a crass approach to relationships and really wants aids to buttress his flagging ability to be self-indulgent. Perhaps Amis is also telling us that twentieth-century human beings are so remote from any sense of connectedness that they are incapable of healing. Such nihilism and solipsism is the hallmark of much artistic expression of the last few decades, with a sense of meaning and shared value attenuated almost to vanishing point. Again the sense of void appears, and with it the implicit cry for fulfilment.

People often need help, not just from the sacramental encounter, but also to learn more about their God-given gifts. Psychology can reveal inner resources we have never acknowledged. In the first place, we have to remember that often people are stunted and blocked by unsatisfactory working situations or living conditions and even the best therapy can find it hard to work against such negative conditions. Again therapy is not magic. Sometimes when people have been disillusioned with the Church they can create high expectations of alternative forms of healing. On the other hand, there are those who reject therapy because they are victims of denial.

Therapy and counselling are not short cuts to solving problems. The process involves time, patience and a will-ingness to enter a trusting relationship with the therapist and, what is vital, a willingness by the person in therapy to see themselves relating in a whole new set of ways to reality. The need for change, for accepting responsibility for our actions, are radical activities that assume a relationship with society that includes accepting responsibility for what is going on around us. A client beginning therapy at a time of crisis cannot expect the process to be one that justifies him- or herself in the face of the rest of life. We may well be victims of malign forces, but why are we victims? Anyone who goes into therapy is not moving into a process of self-justification but rather along a rich road of self-realization.

I believe that with the help of good therapy and counselling we can learn to love ourselves, explore ourselves and celebrate our uniqueness. If our awareness is heightened, we have greater scope for developing our resources and living off situations in a far more creative manner. We can go to work more confidently on the work of art that we are. We cease to accept the negatives and the put-downs. Counselling can give us alternative visions and permissions. It also can promote different perspectives, and enables those de-skilled and downtrodden to be empowered. We can be freed from inertia, stereotypes and cast-iron roles. Men no longer have to act according to received convention and women can escape the structures that have often caused much suffering. The crucial work of getting in touch with our feelings can do untold good in renewing relationships between the sexes. Emotional freedom ensures that energy is not misplaced so as to rise up in negative patterns, but rather enables the mature and open development of the individual.

Counselling and the healing sacraments in the end do share a common purpose: they enable us to engage in life again. The healing work of the sacrament enables us to face the challenge of God to work for the kingdom. If we have encountered justice with mercy and found truth and peace, then we will want to engage in spreading these values in society. I will want others to know of these values and how they change the quality of life. Confession is not wiping the slate clean, but rather a time for new perspectives and new directions. Counselling seems less directive, but by releasing energies and opening up insights it enables us to embark on a more participating style of life. Therapy is not the cultivation of a private landscape, and sacraments are not private religious events connected with narrow individualistic moralism.

The unexamined life is indeed a very thin existence, but an over-introspective lifestyle can be inhibiting. Confession is not a time for fascination with sin or therapy as a re-raking of problems: these are still prison states. It has been said that the greater the healing, the greater the evangelizing process. Finding healing, achieving integration, means that we live and communicate a quality of life that is contagiously life-enhancing.

We live in a world that for all its appeal to choice is very tightly restricted. A few call the tune and set the fashion. So often the unspoken agenda is that this is the way things are and there is no alternative. Allied with hidden agendas, many forms of subtle control exist in society and also in the Church. We need inner freedom and integrity to confront such a world and to be able to show by the energy of our lives that there are alternatives. I believe that the resources of Christianity and the best insights of behavioural sciences give us the dynamism for the counter-culture that has to challenge the received wisdom and often the accepted pessimism.

An important element of Christianity is the spirit of discernment by which we try and read the signs of the times. One keystone of discernment is to look for the fruits of any phenomenon. If the fruits promote charity, enhance life and bring true freedom, then we know that we are encountering the authentic. The joy and attractiveness of primitive Christianity was its ability to offer life-enhancing alternatives. Does the proclamation of the Gospel and its expression in people's lives have that same quality today as it did in the first years of Christianity? The Gospel is always abundant good news but we are the only way that the Good News can be translated into life. There are far too many life-denying proclamations that claim to be the faith but so often these are traditions and not *the* tradition. Every age has to allow the Gospel to speak to its needs, to use imagination resourcefully, and to remember that we are meant to be channels of the Spirit. I believe that the Gospel has this power, but it does need rescuing from paradoxical interpretations.

Epilogue

'Let God be God for you.' So often images and perceptions of God can take over from the reality. It is these partial and perhaps over-filtered images of God that can start us along negative roads. The way society is structured and, as a consequence, the way the Christian community mirrors and echoes society as a whole, can also have a negative effect on us.

As a Carmelite friar I have found in our Order's tradition a positive way forward. In the Rule of St Albert which all Carmelites follow, we are asked to give ourselves to Christ with an undivided heart. The key factor that enables us to follow Christ is meditating on the Scriptures. It is during times of reflection on Scripture that I begin to listen to what God has to say to my heart and also I begin to make connections about what is happening in life. This listening to Scripture is crucial because it allows God to set the agenda. The word of God challenges my preconceptions – my prejudices. Above all, the contemplative attitude that is evoked by listening to God's word in Scripture brings a greater sensitivity to the way in which I listen to others and lets me see a wider range of connections in life. The more I listen the more I become willing to interact with others in a manner that shows respect and sensitivity. I believe that the more we act and react in this way the more we will help each other discover our God-given worth. That sense of our self-worth is crucial to any growth and freedom and it is a basic scriptural message. God has brought us into being out of love and all God's dealings with human beings have been directed towards enabling us to believe we can relate to God in freedom. We are meant to have life in abundance. We can be transformed. The Scriptures show the constant struggle God has to break through to bring this message of creativity and freedom. The prophets, culminating in Jesus, show God the lover trying to penetrate the barriers of formal religion. God wants to speak to our heart. The plea we find in the Prophets is for mercy and a contrite spirit, not ritual and fulfilling legal prescriptions. Wisdom literature in the Bible has the same message in another key: the feminine in God says how it wants to enjoy being with us. Joy, play and, in the Song of Songs, even erotic love are the tones of God's communication with us. In the Christian tradition mystics sing poetically of the loving embraces of God who is tender Father, Mother and so much more. John of the Cross has God speaking as a fascinated lover. The problem is that this abundance of God can seem too much if we feel fragile, and so we react by rejecting intimacy and putting God at a safe distance. Here we have the root of the trouble. This is why prophets and mystics are so crucial down the ages. They keep the memory of God alive and constantly remind us that law can only be lived in the spirit of love. Compassion and forgiveness show the power of God, and in our dealings with each other they are essential if we are to survive. Those of us who live in Britain or Ireland know that only heroic and creative forgiveness will ever heal the wounds of the relationships between the peoples of these islands.

As we allow God to be God for us, and this comes as much by waiting on God as by praying the Scripture, we also change our attitude to God. For many of us God's actions, the way our lives have been shaped, can seem inexplicable. The questions that well up are as many as there are people. Why has marriage come to this? I am dying of cancer, wasting away – why have my worst fears been realized? My children never bother with me or the Church. Why? I am gay and pressures and ambiguities are loaded on to me, and I experience hurt because of prejudice and sheer ignorance. Why is this? All of these reactions point to a latent anger that can boil away and find no expression. Can we be angry with God? Can we forgive God?

I believe that if we are going to find freedom we need to express our feelings to God and find healing. In that willingness to say out aloud what we feel and say how we have suffered we can begin to make sense of our lives. What we have in common with God is our woundedness. I have been helped to find some focus here in the writings of Jean Vanier. Jean Vanier is the founder of the L'Arche communities that care for the severely mentally disabled. The inspiration is that the carers and those they care for heal each other. Jean Vanier reminds us that Jesus saved us when utterly broken. The Jesus of the way of the cross and Calvary was physically and in every way derelict and broken. I believe that when I come to God feeling bewildered and hurt, I pray to a God who in Christ has come to the brink of human brokenness and feels with us as one of us. I believe that because of the woundedness of God in Christ, I can communicate and we can forgive each other.

But what about our relations with one another? How can society, how can the Church be healed and transformed? Much is wrong with the way we live now and the call goes out to the Church to do its bit to improve matters. However, the physician needs to be healed. The Church in its pilgrim journey is ever in need of reformation and yet it is the light of the world and the place where we meet Christ. But the light and the meetings with Christ depend on the mediation of fragile vulnerable human beings. There is, as I have indicated, the constant tension between what the law requires and where people are. What is vital is that we live the law so that it is interpreted with loving respect for those who struggle or who feel trapped in complex situations.

It is all too easy to dismiss people because we are too busy, or because we think we know how the law is to be interpreted. I remember hearing of a couple who went along to see a parish priest. They wanted to get married. The woman was a deeply committed Catholic but the man she wanted to marry was divorced. They went to her priest to ask if a petition for nullity could be started. He refused, very abruptly: 'It is quite a clear case, black and white, no chance at all.' Not only did they feel rejected but, as the man was black, the priest's thoughtless remark about black and white felt like an insult. Fortunately, I was able to refer the couple to the appropriate authorities and they are now happily married. The hurt inflicted was unnecessary.

As I have been writing this book, the Pope has promulgated his encyclical *Veritatis Splendor*. This is an important document that gives a timely reminder of the existence of objective morality. There are basic principles and we cannot live by moral relativism. *Veritatis Splendor*, like all encyclicals, is addressed to the bishops and it will be their role to unpack this weighty document. A first reading shows it to be rooted in a profound meditation on Scripture but there is also a great deal of philosophical analysis. It is a serious document that will merit careful and respectful study. However it is interpreted and made accessible to people at large, it is vital that in the interpretation people's struggles will be accepted. It is not a case of denying objective morality or asking for a shift in the goalposts. Rather, I would ask that those who are in second marriages or who struggle with some area of personal morality will not feel that a door has been slammed in their face. In his novels Graham Greene speaks of the awful mercy of God. His characters, like Pinkie in *Brighton Rock*, the petty criminal who carries his personal hell around with him, or Scobie in *The Heart of the Matter*, who sins out of pity, in terms of objective morality die in mortal sin and are alienated from God. Greene however always wants to leave us with a little hope as regards the ultimate destiny of these characters. In this I would hold that Greene like Christ is praying that the sinner should not die but be able to be touched by Christ's channelling of the Father's mercy.

The Church must teach with authority and in doing that continues Christ's mission. However, Christ's teaching with authority was not something coercive but, rather, it was based on the clarity and directness of his message. People were challenged, liberated, but not burdened. He empowered people to move from paralysis, he helped people see the way forward. He gave a vision of living by love and he was himself that love incarnate. He also enabled those who caused the structural sin of the day to change. He gave ordinary people permission to feel they had a share in God's project. Prostitute, publican and fisherman were all given the chance to be more than their role and their social conditioning. Christ was vehemently against those who in the name of God imposed burdens, so we should be careful not to make salvation possible only for an élite. The Kingdom of God is not about the nice, the safe and the pious.

I feel strongly that the Church must be, as Pope John Paul II once said, an expert in humanity. Society needs a force for compassion at a time when complexity and uncertainty can make people fearful and insecure. But, above all, if we are to survive we must be people who support each other and show great care. I would like to end by making a modest proposal towards healing our society.

All of us need help in our journey through life, and yet so often we can live separate or parallel existences. I would like to see for the good of society, but also for a greater mutuality, deeper trust and collaboration between the priest/minister and the counsellor/therapist. The religious dimension in a person's problems can be either a creative force for healing or the cause of the suffering and here the minister has something to offer. Conversely the therapist has skills that the minister could well respect and adapt, especially the non-directive approach. I believe that minister and therapist need to give each other much more mutual support. If a priest is involved with people's needs and problems he can be overwhelmed by what he hears. Priests are asked for help in so many areas where perhaps we can intuit but that is about as far as we can go. In our dealings with people our feelings often cloud judgement or we unconsciously impose a personal vision as reality. I have come to realize that the minister, just as much as anyone who cares for people, needs supervision. It is also important to look for some objective assessment to help us evaluate what we have been doing. We also need to examine our feelings and ascertain how appropriate our behaviour has been towards the people who come to see us. I need others to help my vision and to get me to be honest about my way of behaving. As a helper or adviser I can easily end up playing God. Someone needs to remind me who I am. On the other hand, the minister can help the therapist, not only by collaborating where appropriate, but by listening to the needs of the person who has as the core of their work such intense dealings with brokenness. Creativity, energy, consistency, objectivity, these qualities have to be deeply rooted in a self constantly seeking understanding. Where the therapist is linked to a religious tradition there he or she should be enabled to drink from wellsprings of life. Sometimes as a priest I find that the most important help I can give is to enable others to begin to re-image God and move away from vengeful theories of atonement.

When I began my theological studies in Rome in 1960, the first lecture I attended was on the Trinity. The lecturer was a Catalan Carmelite, Bartolomao Xiberta. Lectures were in Latin but one phrase stuck in my mind — the Trinity was about relationships. Life for me is about relationships, family, my community, my friends — if society is to change, we need deep healing in the way we relate at whatever level. This book has, I hope, been a small contribution towards that project. The alternative is the lonely detached individual whose theme song is 'I'll do it my way'. It is the figure from the Western, riding out into the sunset, having come from nowhere to cause (sometimes beneficial) mayhem and then travel on. The lonely detached thinker keeps appearing in various guises. He is the romantic poet, the pioneer, the scientist and now perhaps the computer programmer answerable only to his terminal. I notice too that this lonely individual is always a man.

This isolated individual is hardly a model for humanity, and in his isolation gives no sign of being designed for relationships. We are unique and irreplaceable, but our highest achievement is our ability to love. We are meant to transcend our basic biological needs and yet never to deny them their due. We need each other to survive, but our existence must always be more than survival. Created, we mirror our Creator by our creativity: limited, we nonetheless know our future lies beyond space and time. We are animal and yet we can connect with angels. As I write I become aware of another remark from my days studying with Father Xiberta. Christianity is about mystery, it cannot be confined in a simple statement. Jesus is both God and man. The divine and the human make up that person who is Christ. The whole of our life therefore should be allowing the marvellous tension of the divine and the human to flourish. Our human nature is wonderful because God could become one of us, but we are only really human when we allow the gift of God to find freedom in us. The insight of our dignity and the wonderful way God graces us needs to be broadcast as powerfully as possible to our society. That is why I hope that the Church as it exercises its teaching mission will always show its expertise in understanding humanity and never allow a style of teaching or a tone of voice to cloud the glory of what it has to say. Finally, I would like to believe that we can all accept our fragility and limitations and yet realize that we are God's work of art, and so collaborate in allowing a fulfilment that goes beyond our dreams to break out in us.

Books consulted
or for further reading

Peter Brown, *The Body and Society* (Faber and Faber, London, 1990)

Denise Lardner Carmody, *Virtuous Woman* (Orbis Books, Maryknoll, NY, 1992)

John Carmody, *Towards a Male Spirituality* (Twenty-Third Publications, Mystic, CT, 1989)

Joann Wolski Conn, *Women's Spirituality – Resources for Christian Development* (Paulist Press, Mahwah, NJ, 1986)

Bernard Cooke, *Reconciled Sinners* (Twenty-Third Publications, Mystic, CT, 1986)

Gabriel Daly OSA, *Creation and Redemption* (Gill and Macmillan, Dublin, 1988)

Donal Dorr, *The Social Justice Agenda* (Gill and Macmillan, Dublin, 1991)

Mary Gordon, *Final Payments* (Black Swan, London, 1987; originally Hamish Hamilton, London, 1978)

Mary Gordon, *The Company of Women* (Black Swan, London, 1987; originally Jonathan Cape, London, 1980)

Mary Grey, *Redeeming the Dream* (SPCK, London, 1989)

Mary Grey, *The Wisdom of Fools?* (SPCK, London, 1993)

Kevin T. Kelly, *New Directions in Moral Theology* (Geoffrey Chapman, London, 1992)

John Mahoney, *The Making of Moral Theology* (Clarendon Press, Oxford, 1987)

Martin E. Marty and R. Scott Appleby, *The Glory and the Power: The Fundamentalist Challenge to the Modern World* (Beacon Press, Boston, 1992)

Gareth Moore, *The Body in Context* (SCM Press, London, 1992)

Elaine Pagels, *Adam, Eve and the Serpent* (Penguin Books, London, 1990)

Sandra M. Schneiders, *Beyond Patching* (Paulist Press, Mahwah, NJ, 1991)

Peter Selby, *Liberating God* (SPCK, London, 1983)

Gerard S. Sloyan, *Catholic Morality Revisited* (Twenty-Third Publications, Mystic, CT, 1990)